HANS CHRISTIAN ANDERSEN
and his world

REGINALD SPINK

HANS CHRISTIAN
ANDERSEN

and his world

THAMES AND HUDSON
LONDON

In writing this book I have drawn chiefly on Danish
sources. I am indebted in particular to the following
writers and Andersen scholars: Edvard Collin, Rigmor
Stampe, Elith Reumert, G.L.Wad, Hans Brix, H.G.
Olrik, Hjalmar Helweg, Paul V. Rubow, H. Topsøe-
Jensen, Fredrik Böök, Svend Larsen, Bo Grønbech,
Erling Nielsen, Elias Bredsdorff and Erik Dal. A
special word of thanks is due to Dr Bredsdorff and Dr
Dal for personal interest and encouragement. Any
errors of commission, omission, emphasis or interpreta-
tion are mine.   R.S.

Printed in Great Britain by Jarrold and Sons Ltd, Norwich

ISBN 0 500 13038 8

That 'the child is father of the man', in Wordsworth's well-known phrase, can scarcely have been more sharply illustrated than in the life and career of Hans Christian Andersen. Heredity and his early environment clearly determined Andersen's personality. He himself was fascinated and obsessed by the fact all his life. Recollections of childhood and youth, sometimes idealized and transmuted, often only thinly disguised as fiction, inform almost everything that he wrote. They are the principal themes of his three autobiographies; they inspired the novels through which he first became internationally famous, his many plays and poems, and above all many of the celebrated fairy tales, those simple-seeming but many-levelled and stylistically sophisticated masterpieces, written, he insisted, for readers of all ages: 'Children understood only the trappings', he said.

As nearly everyone knows, Andersen was the son of a shoe-maker. He could never forget this humble birth, but alternately bewailed and gloried in it. To be born in a duckyard and, despite every contrary indication, prove that you are a swan can be an achievement at the best of times. When breeding, and the academic education dependent on it, are all-important, as they were at the time and in the society into which Hans Christian Andersen was born, it is a truly remarkable one.

Odense in 1805

5

Odense in 1811, showing St Knud's Church where Andersen was confirmed

Probably Hans Andersen the shoemaker was not very proficient at his craft. Certainly he was not very successful at it, for the family lived poorly, though shoemaking, more than cobbling or repairing, was a skilled occupation. He was intelligent, however, and in an age with little general schooling had got himself at least the elements of an education, and for his class was well read. At the same time he was a dreamer, undoubtedly neurotic, and embittered by frustrated ambitions. He held vaguely radical views in politics, and in religion was a free-thinker. 'Christ was a man like us, but an exceptional man,' he once said. And: 'There is no Devil but the one in our own hearts.' Slight of build, round-faced and ruddy, in Andersen's description of him, he was twenty-three at the time of his marriage, and his wife was thirty-eight. Hans Christian, who was their only child, was born two months after the wedding.

It was a happy marriage, Andersen said, and despite the romantic gloss which he tended to put on his childhood in later years, there is no reason to suppose otherwise. But the shoemaker and his wife were ill-matched in many other respects besides age. She had the rough, raw-boned physique of a peasant. She was practically illiterate, able to read block letters with difficulty but unable to write. Where he was a rationalist, she was highly superstitious. Andersen says that she was 'ignorant of the world and of life'. But if ignorant in the educational sense, she certainly was not without worldly experience. Six years before Hans Christian was born she had given birth to an illegitimate daughter. The father, a journey-

6

man potter, had deserted her and the baby had been put out to nurse. Andersen is unlikely to have known this half-sister as a child.

Anne Marie was illegitimate herself, one of three daughters her mother had borne to three different men, all out of wedlock. Andersen called on one of these half-aunts soon after his arrival in Copenhagen, but failed to get any help from her. If only her half-sister, Hans Christian's mother, had sent her a little girl, he records her as having said. The lady, in short, ran a brothel. Fears that these disreputable relations might one day turn up to embarrass him used to haunt Andersen in the years of his success and social respectability. None of them did, however, except that on one occasion during the last years of his life his half-sister and her lover called on him discreetly to beg money, and she turned out to be, not, as he had feared, a prostitute, but a respectable if wretchedly poor washerwoman. Andersen's mother would eventually become a washerwoman herself, but during his childhood she was a happy and houseproud wife as well as an affectionate mother, determined to see that her son got a better start in life than she had had. As a child, she had once been sent out to beg.

Original illustration by Vilhelm Pedersen of the fairy tale *She Was Good for Nothing*, in which Andersen's mother is the washerwoman

Odense in the 1840's. Munkemølle-stræde, where Andersen lived as a child, adjoined the square on the right

Andersen says in his autobiographies that his father's people had been well-to-do farmers, but had been impoverished by cattle disease and by a fire that had destroyed their home. His grand-father's mind had given way under the strain and the family had been forced to move into the town, where Andersen's father had been reluctantly apprenticed to a shoemaker, instead of being decently educated as they had intended. Apart from the grand-father's mental disability, however, the story is untrue; he, too, had been a shoemaker. The account of the farm and its disasters was pure fantasy, probably invented, and afterwards believed in, by Andersen's grandmother, who also claimed that her own grand-mother had belonged to an aristocratic German family and had eloped with a strolling player. She, too, in fact, was of humble Danish descent. In spite of these harmless fantasies, Andersen's paternal grandmother was, of all his immediate ancestors, probably the most normal. A kindly, busy, blue-eyed little woman, she maintained herself and her witless husband by tending the garden of the local poor-law institution, where in time he would become an inmate.

Andersen remembered this grandfather as a wild-eyed old man who made artistically carved figures of birds, beasts and grotesquely-headed men which he peddled in the countryside, and who sometimes walked down the street decked with flowers and wearing a paper hat, singing strangely as he went. Hans Christian would slink terrified into a doorway till the old man and the jeering mob of urchins at his heels had gone by. He could never rid himself of the fear that he might one day end up like this grandfather. 'I knew I was of his flesh and blood,' he writes; and studying himself in the glass during his depressed later years, he seemed to see a resemblance. There were many times when he behaved more than a little oddly himself; but a tougher side of his nature, derived doubtless from his mother, invariably asserted itself in the end, together with the magnificent sense of humour which enabled him to laugh even at his own quirks and strange moods.

The exact birthplace of Hans Christian Andersen, at Odense on 2 April 1805, is uncertain. It is no more than an oral, and rather tenuous, tradition that he was born in the house, called H.C. Andersens Hus, which together with a massive modern annexe now forms the Andersen museum, full of personal relics and editions of his works in every language, and in the summer packed with milling crowds of tourists. It seems unlikely that his parents lived together at all until the year after his birth, and when he was two years old they moved to a cottage a few streets away. This is the house in Munkemøllestræde, now carefully restored to its original

The traditional birthplace of Hans Christian Andersen at Odense; lithograph, 1868

9

Odense Gaol (on the left) as it was when Andersen was a boy

From the home in Munkemøllestræde as it is today

condition, and little visited by the uninitiated, that he describes so lovingly in *The Fairy Tale of My Life*:

One small room that was almost taken up by the shoemaker's work-bench, the bed, and the settle where I used to sleep, was my childhood home. But the walls were hung with pictures; pretty cups, glasses and ornaments stood on the chest of drawers; and above the work-bench over by the window was a shelf of books and ballads. Over the food cupboard in the little kitchen hung the rack of pewter plates; this little room seemed to me big and grand. The door itself, with its landscapes painted on the panels, meant to me then as much as a whole picture gallery now. From the kitchen, with the help of a ladder, you got on to the roof, where, in the gutter between our house and the neighbour's, was a box of soil with chives and parsley, my mother's entire garden; it flourishes still in my fairy tale 'The Snow Queen'.

Andersen's father had few friends and he used to spend most of his leisure with his son, on whom he doted. On winter Sundays he made toys and paper cut-outs for him, and read aloud from *A Thousand and One Nights*, Lafontaine's fables and the plays of Ludvig Holberg, 'the Molière of the North'. In summer they went to the woods, where Hans Christian gathered wild strawberries or made daisy chains, while his father sat abstracted on the grass. Once a year, when the beech-trees sprang out in May, his mother would put on her best patterned dress and go with them.

A very early memory, and one which left a lasting impression on the boy's mind, was of a visit to the local gaol, where Hans Christian's parents knew the janitor. The occasion was a family party. The visitors were admitted through the iron-studded gate, which was locked behind them with a rattle of keys. Two of the prisoners waited on them. But the horrified child refused to touch any of the good things that were set before them. Thinking he was unwell, his mother laid him on the bed, where he lay listening feverishly to the sound, real or imagined, of the convicts as they sang at their spinning wheels. It was a rough night, and the wind lashed

(*Above*) The house where Andersen
spent his childhood; a watercolour
done in 1836

(*Below*) The river and mill (right)
near Andersen's home; 1831

at the boy's face when they carried him home. The gaol held a dreadful fascination for him after that visit. It figures vividly in Andersen's novel *O.T.*

At the beginning of the nineteenth century, Denmark was a larger force in the world than she is today. Her absolutist king, Christian VII, ruled over Norway, Iceland and the duchies of Schleswig and Holstein. Before the Napoleonic Wars she was a considerable naval power. Odense, situated almost in the centre, was at that time the second city. But it had only 5,000 inhabitants, and compared with Copenhagen, the capital, eighty-five miles to the east, it was in many ways old-fashioned, clinging to ancient traditions and still subject to the guild system. The shoemaker would occasionally take his son to watch the guild processions as they passed through the streets with their waving flags and banners. Detachments of soldiers used to march through the town, playing their pipes. There would be wrestling matches between sailors in the harbour. At Shrovetide, the butchers' company paraded the streets, dragging a fattened ox wreathed with flowers. Andersen's mother claimed a distant relationship with the red-nosed harlequin who used to perform, in cap and bells, on such occasions.

A more dramatic incursion took place in 1808. In September of the previous year, the British had bombarded Copenhagen and carried off the Danish fleet in order to prevent it from being seized by the French. This had driven Denmark into an alliance with Napoleon; and now a French army, supported by Spanish auxiliaries, marched through Denmark to invade Sweden, Britain's one remaining ally at the time. Arriving in Odense, they encamped in the market place and in the ruins of one of the town's churches. There was a great deal of commotion, with much firing of guns.

French and Spanish troops in Denmark in 1808

Hans Christian was only three years old at the time, but he retained vivid memories, probably kept alive by family reminders, of rather mutinous Spaniards, one of whom was led away to be executed after, it was said, killing a Frenchman. One day a Spanish soldier picked the boy up and, to his mother's horror, pressed a silver image, a crucifix no doubt, to his lips.

Under the Treaty of Kiel, which brought the war to an end in 1814, Denmark was forced to cede Norway to Sweden. The Danish crown prince, Christian Frederik, who had been vice-regent, and for a brief interlude king, of Norway, now came to reside, as provincial governor, at Odense. He held court in the stately eighteenth-century palace in the town centre. This tiny royal city exhibited the most marked contrasts. There were some fashionable houses in elegant streets. Civil and military officials met with well-to-do merchants in exclusive clubs. Concerts were given for them in the town hall, and there was also a theatre, presenting a mainly German repertoire. A wide gulf separated this élite from the rest of the townspeople, consisting mostly of artisans and

The British bombardment of Copenhagen, 3-4 September 1807; painting by C. V. Eckersberg

The canal at Odense

labourers, who occupied romantic-looking but tumble-down half-timbered houses in dark alleys and narrow side-streets. This was the world of the shoemaker and his family.

During these early years, Hans Christian spent a fair amount of his time under the care of his grandmother in the grounds of the institution, which included a mental department. He listened with mixed feelings of fear and curiosity to the rambling speech and strange songs of the harmless cases he would meet in the grounds. One day he ventured inside. The building was divided by a long corridor, with cubicles on either side of it. Peering through a chink in one of the doors, he could just discern the figure of a half-naked woman, her hair hanging loose over her shoulders. She was singing in what seemed a rather beautiful voice; but hearing a scraping sound outside, she flew screaming at the door, and thrust out her arm through a hatch which sprang open at the top. The attendant found Hans Christian crouched in a fainting condition at its foot.

The boy used to help his grandmother to burn the garden rubbish, on great bonfires that are recalled in the fairy tale 'The Fir Tree'. He also accompanied her into the spinning room, where he was soon entertaining the old women with scraps of information he had picked up, giving on one occasion an elementary anatomy lesson on the blackboard. They, for their part, entertained him with the old ballads which they sang, and the folk tales they told, as they worked: traditional songs and tales that had been transmitted orally

(*Above*) Odense Theatre

The charity school at Odense

down the years. These childhood memories were stored away in his impressionable and imaginative mind, and formed with others the raw material of many of the future fairy tales.

For a short time the boy attended a dame school in Odense, later a school for small boys. A solitary child, younger than most of his schoolfellows, he rarely joined in their games, but sat during play-time in the classroom. The evenings he spent amusing himself with the playthings his father made for him: puppets and peepshows, working models of mills and the like. In summer he would sit in the yard behind the cottage, making clothes for his puppets, erecting a tent with his mother's aprons, or gazing into the solitary gooseberry bush, studying the buds and watching the unfolding leaves. His imagination was stimulated, too, by a visit to the theatre with his parents.

Suddenly a chance presented itself to improve the family fortunes. A local manor wanted a shoemaker for regular employment on the estate. A cottage would be provided in the village, with a garden and a cow. So Hans Christian's father set out eagerly for the big house, taking with him a pair of dancing shoes that he had been instructed to make as a test piece from silk provided by the manor but using his own leather. All the little family's brightest hopes went with him. In the evening he returned bitter and crestfallen; the lady of the house had declared the shoes useless. All three were dissolved in tears. Life went on as in the past, except that the shoemaker grew increasingly silent and morose.

The rear of the cottage in Munke-møllestræde as it is today: 'only one gooseberry bush, but it is as good as many'

The tide of war sweeping through Germany now drew closer again to Denmark, as the invincible Napoleon, the shoemaker's hero, carried everything before him. Hans Christian's father suddenly announced a dramatic decision; he would volunteer for the militia, which was about to depart from Odense to link up with Denmark's French allies in Germany. Enthusiasm for the 'liberator' was probably a less powerful motive in this decision than social ambitions and economic considerations. At any rate, he was paid by a conscript to take his place, a procedure permitted by the regulations, and he spoke confidently of being able to better his position when he returned as a lieutenant. In the event, the regiment had got no further than Holstein when peace was signed, and the shoemaker was back at his bench. But his health had begun to decline, and soon, it would seem, his mental faculties also. In 1816, he fell into a delirious fever and rambled away about Napoleon.

Riverside scene at Odense, 1816

His wife's typical reaction was to dispatch Hans Christian, on foot, some four or five miles into the country to call a woman quack. She made some passes over the boy, tied a woollen thread round his wrist and gave him a leaf of buckthorn (a cathartic). 'Will my father die?' he asked. 'If he dies,' she replied, 'you will meet his ghost on the way home.' Three days later the shoemaker was dead. They buried him in the paupers' corner of the churchyard. Hans Christian, now eleven, was transferred to the charity school.

The shoemaker's widow had started going out as a washer-woman, leaving Hans Christian after school hours to his own devices. After a while, it was decided that he should be found work; 'not for the money's sake, but to keep him out of mischief'. He got a job at a cloth mill, but did not in fact do very much work there, as the men soon found that he had a good voice and could sing and tell stories to them while they worked. Their horseplay and coarse jests, however, upset the sensitive lad and in a very short time his mother took him away and sent him instead to a small tobacco factory where, again, his singing and improvised songs appealed to his workmates. But his mother soon removed him, as it seemed that the tobacco might be affecting his health.

Two years after her husband's death, Anne Marie married again. Her second husband, like the first, was a shoemaker, and like him was younger than herself. He was a more successful craftsman, however, and before long the family had moved to a better house, which had a strip of garden, planted with fruit bushes, running down to the river. Here there was a water-mill with a lock and three great wheels. It was a new and exciting playground, and the boy

18

would wade barefoot into the muddy water when the river-bed emptied, catch fishes with his hands and watch the water-rats and other wild-life by the riverside. The experiences are graphically recalled in the fairy tale 'The Steadfast Tin Soldier'.

At the bottom of the garden Hans Christian found another platform from which to display his talents, and he also found a new, and better, audience. In the river lay a large boulder, on which his mother pounded the family linen after washing it in the stream. On this boulder the boy would stand and sing at the top of his voice. He had found out that there were listeners in the richer house next door, and that fashionable visitors, sitting in the garden, were beginning to talk of his voice. Praise, which he often canvassed, stimulated Hans Christian Andersen to better effort all his life, as he frequently admitted; just as criticism, however silly and trivial, could plunge him into bouts of the deepest despondency. And so he sang and recited, and soon his musical voice became the talk of Odense. To the boy himself it seemed as if his Aladdin's lamp had started to shine, and in rhapsodic moments he imagined some prince

The place where Andersen's mother did her washing

In Memory of Little Maria's Death, a poem written when Andersen was nearly twelve; the earliest existing manuscript

of China ascending from the Odense river to take him in triumph to the emperor's palace down below.

The boy's future now came under debate. His stepfather declined to interfere, or show any interest. His mother fancied him as a tailor, and argued that, in that occupation, he would never be short of remnants for dressing his puppets. His grandmother, cherishing superior ideas as always, thought he was cut out for office work. As for Hans Christian himself, he was set on becoming an actor. He had long cultivated the friendship of a billman, and had managed with his help to get behind the scenes at the theatre. His eagerness and intelligence, and the persistence that would remain characteristic of him, got him a couple of walking-on parts. On one magical occasion he was given a line or two to speak.

Back-stage talk about the glamours of theatrical life in Copenhagen worked on his imagination, and already he saw himself achieving fame and fortune there. The knowledge that the lady next door had been an actress stimulated his singing and reciting on the washing boulder.

As news of this gifted child got around the town, various people began to take a benevolent interest in him: to lend him books, and invite him into their homes, where he would declaim scenes from Holberg and other authors. One of the more influential of these early benefactors was a Colonel Høegh-Guldberg. He had business at the palace and (if it sounds like a fairy tale we have to remember that this small town was the second city in a benevolent autocracy) he recommended the boy to the crown prince, who granted him an audience. Christian Frederik – he was to become Christian VIII in 1839 – received him graciously and questioned him about his ambitions. The colonel had advised him to say that he was anxious to get a better education, and he dutifully did so, while hastening to add that his real ambition was to go on the stage. But in order to make good in that profession, the prince suggested, you had to be a genius, and he thought it would be better, first, to learn a trade. When he had done that, he promised to help him.

The interview, at which Hans Christian had both sung and recited, was deeply disappointing, but he could never be deflected from his set course for long. He begged and pleaded with his mother to allow him to try his luck in Copenhagen. 'Whatever will become of you?' she asked. 'I shall become famous,' he replied; 'first you go through a cruel time, and then you become famous.' In the end she yielded, but only after she had consulted a fortune-teller. 'He will become a great man,' the woman declared, after studying cards and coffee grounds, 'and Odense will be illuminated in his honour.'

Hans Christian emptied his money-box and his mother packed his few things into a bundle. The driver of the mailcoach was bribed to pick the boy up after starting and set him down outside the gates of Copenhagen. And, early one autumn morning, the coach rumbled over the cobblestones through the town gates. His mother and grandmother, in tears, were there to see him off (he would never see his grandmother again), and the great adventure began. After crossing the Great Belt, in a choppy sea, on the mail-boat, he continued his journey by coach to the metropolis. He knew nobody there, but from one of his local benefactors he had begged a letter of introduction to the leading ballerina, the famous Madame Schall. The theatre season had just opened when he reached Copenhagen on Monday morning, 6 September 1819. He was barely fourteen and a half years old.

(*Above*) The old centre of Odense
when Andersen lived there as a child

(*Right*) Andersen's departure for
Copenhagen; modern fresco by
Larsen Stevns

(*Opposite*) Anna Margrethe Schall
(1775–1852) in the title role of
Galeotti's ballet *Nina*

After installing himself at a cheap inn, he made his first pilgrimage to the theatre, and then lost no time in seeking out the admired ballerina at her home. She had never heard of her correspondent, but she admitted the boy – he could hardly have been kept out – and he proceeded to demonstrate his talents. He had put on his best, ill-fitting clothes for the occasion, but now he took off his outsize boots and, placing them in a corner of the room, performed in his stockinged feet. He chose to improvise a scene from a play that he had seen in Odense, and he sang and danced, using his tall hat for a tambourine. More startled than impressed by his awkward performance, and concluding that he must be a little mad, the lady hastened to get rid of him. When he burst into tears, she promised to put in a word for him at the theatre, and said he could call occasionally at her house for a meal (an offer he never availed himself of).

With his usual extraordinary persistence, Hans Christian then sought other interviews, and eventually succeeded, without any sort of introduction, in gaining admittance to the theatre's director. Rather more brutally than Madame Schall, he said that he could

The gallery at the theatre in Copenhagen

only take on people with an education. His savings spent, the boy was soon in financial trouble. Either he would have to return to Odense, and make himself a laughing-stock, or he must take the advice of many well-wishers and work at some trade in Copenhagen. As the latter seemed the more sensible alternative, he arranged, subject to provision of satisfactory testimonials, to get engaged as an apprentice joiner. But he left the job after the first day's employment, owing to the same sort of horseplay that had upset him at the factory in Odense.

At this point, he suddenly bethought himself of his voice, which everyone in Odense had praised but which nobody in Copenhagen, except for Madame Schall, had heard. He remembered having read in the paper at home about the appointment of a new director at the theatre's song school, an immigrant Italian opera-singer, Giuseppe Siboni. So he made straight for Siboni's house, and as usual was admitted. Siboni happened on that very evening to be entertaining some distinguished members of the Copenhagen literary and musical world at dinner, and, in a convivial mood, they streamed into the hall to view the 'oddity' that had been announced.

Their applause for the boy's singing and reciting was perhaps at first ironical, but warming to his eagerness and sincerity they agreed to help him. Siboni himself would give him lessons in singing. One of his guests, C.E.F. Weyse, a composer, whose fine settings of Danish songs are still popular, opened a subscription list for him. Hans Christian wept for joy, and wrote his first, rapturous letter home.

He now spent much of his time in Siboni's house, being taught, listening to practices, getting free meals, and in return running errands and making himself generally useful. At the end of six months, however, the singing lessons came to an end, partly because Hans Christian's voice had broken; Siboni felt that he could make no further progress with him. Other well-wishers had meanwhile been giving him free lessons in Danish, German and Latin; others again in dancing and acting. Various people lent him books. Another subscription list saved him from having to go home. Then, in September 1820, about a year after his arrival in the capital, he managed to get a walking-on part at the theatre. More followed, and in April of the following year he was given the small part of a gnome, and saw his name in print for the first time, in the programme. He was admitted to the song school in the same month. At about this time, too, he submitted his first play, anonymously, to the theatre; it was pronounced unusable, being full of elementary mistakes of grammar and spelling. In May 1822 he was finally discharged from the theatre. During most of this period he had lived very poorly in a windowless room in one of the more

(*Opposite*) The street where Andersen lodged during his first years in Copenhagen

Slagelse in the nineteenth century

disreputable parts of the city. In the evening, he used to open the back door to admit an elderly man who came 'for supper' with his 'daughter' in the room above. 'I was in the midst of Copenhagen's mysteries, and did not know how to read them.'

Three years had now passed since Hans Christian's arrival in the capital, and his situation was again beginning to be desperate. Should he take the advice proffered by nearly everybody, and go home to work at a trade? He must surely have given the idea serious consideration. However, once again his perseverance was rewarded. Another play, a tragedy, had been submitted and rejected like the previous one as utterly unsuitable. This time, though, the rejection was accompanied by the encouraging comment that the author might one day produce something of value, if he could first be given an education. This heart-warming observation may have been inspired by a senior government official, Jonas Collin, a member of the theatre's governing body and later its director. At any rate, Collin applied for and secured a royal grant with which to pay for Andersen's education, and made all the arrangements for it.

The educational establishment chosen by Collin was the state grammar school at Slagelse, a small town some ninety miles to the south-west of Copenhagen, in the same island. Andersen was seventeen when he went there in October 1822, and was the oldest

(*Opposite*) Jonas Collin (1776–1861)

28

Simon Meisling

(*Below*) The grammar school at Slagelse

Til **Examen Artium** i October 1828 har fremstillet sig
Hans Christian Andersen, og paa Grund
af de specielle Characterer for

Udarbeidelse i Modersmaalet................................. *Haud*
Latin... *N. sont.*
Latinsk Stiil.. *Haud*
Græsk... *Haud*
Hebraisk.. *Haud*
Religion... *Haud*
Geographie... *Haud*
Historie... *Haud*
Arithmetik.. *Haud*
Geometrie.. *Haud*
Tydsk... *Laud*
Fransk... *Haud*

erholdt Hoved-Characteer *Haud illaudabilis*

Kiöbenhavn d. 22. *Oct* 18 28.

Dette bevidnes herved af undertegnede

H. Oehlenschläger

det Philos. Facultets Decanus.

Andersen's examination certificate

boy in his form, the others being all aged twelve and thirteen. The newly appointed headmaster was Simon Meisling, a classical scholar and translator of Shakespeare, then about thirty-five. Meisling's translations of Greek and Latin poetry are highly regarded, and he was something of a minor poet himself. But he failed completely to understand Andersen's tense and hypersensitive nature, and, while supplying Collin with extremely favourable reports of the youth's progress, mocked and bullied him disgracefully. His slatternly wife tried to seduce Andersen after they had persuaded him, probably for the money, to move from his lodgings in town into their own house. Andersen spent a miserable three years in this squalid household, feeling frequently in suicidal mood. When Meisling was transferred to Elsinore, a more attractive town that was nearer to the capital, the object of his own frustrated ambitions, Andersen went with him. There, in the following year, a sympathetic master took up the boy's case with Collin, who had him removed from the school and given private tuition in Copenhagen. In October of that year, 1828, Andersen, now twenty-three,

St Nicholas Church in Copenhagen

passed his university entrance examination, and Collin got his grant extended for a further year.

Released from restraint, the sensitive plant began to unfold. On the advice of Collin and other well-wishers, Andersen, on the whole, had abstained from writing while at school, so as to concentrate on his studies. But he had written a few poems, one of which, 'The Dying Child', was published in a literary magazine. The classically trained Meisling had ridiculed its new romantic fervency, but its qualities of lyricism and sincerity have kept it permanently in Danish anthologies, together with a few of Andersen's later lyrics, though the bulk of his large subsequent output of verse is largely forgotten. In the meantime, his second rejected play and a melo-dramatic tale, left with a printer before going to Slagelse, had been published, probably by this time against his wishes. The small book

32

was entitled *Youthful Attempts*, by 'William Christian Walter', a pseudonym coupling his own forename with those of his heroes, Shakespeare and Scott. His examination now safely behind him, however, he embarked on a period of intensive literary activity. His darkest hours seemed to be over; his splendid humour began to assert itself.

Andersen's first significant work appeared in 1829. Whimsically entitled *A Walking Tour from Holmens Canal to the Eastern Point of Amager* (it was a walk he made daily across Copenhagen to his tutor's), the book is an entertaining collection of capricious incidents and inventions in the manner of the German romantic writer E. T. A. Hoffmann; and although immature and over-literary, it foreshadows the fairy tales at their gayest and wittiest. It was quickly followed by the production, at the theatre he had wooed with such a determined attack, of *Love on St Nicholas Church Tower*, a play in verse parodying the heroic style of Schiller. His first volume of poems came out the year after. All three works were critical and financial successes. His faith in himself, and the trust of the benefactors who had sponsored him, had proved justified.

Flushed with success, Andersen decided in the summer of 1830 to see more of Denmark and visit places he had chosen as the setting for a projected historical novel in the style of Walter Scott. Armed with letters of introduction from Collin, he took ship for Jutland, and found that his fame had gone before him, his arrival being reported in the local papers. Before returning to Copenhagen, he spent three weeks at Odense, basking in the warmth of his success and being proudly shown off to all and sundry by his mother. He then travelled south to Fåborg, in the same island, in order to stay with a fellow-student, Christian Voigt, the son of a well-to-do merchant. Christian's pretty, brown-eyed sister, Riborg, aged twenty, was at home and blushingly served tea for him when he arrived. Although loosely engaged to a local forestry student, she seemed attracted to Andersen, and he certainly was by her. She spoke admiringly of his *Walking Tour* and his poems; they strolled in the woods together; and when she saw him off on the coach she gave him a posy. When she came to Copenhagen, a few months later, he pressed into her hand a slip of paper containing a poem, 'To Her'. A charming little lyric, which has remained in the anthologies (and was set to music by Delius), it began: 'Thought of my thought'. It was a declaration of love.

What happened next will always be something of a mystery. Andersen was undoubtedly in love with the girl, and in spite of her prior 'engagement' she was almost certainly drawn to him. Given only a little of the determination which Andersen displayed in most other respects, she might have accepted him. Instead, in a long letter

33

Riborg Voigt

(*Opposite*) Andersen as a young man

in which he again declared his love for her, he virtually renounced his claims in favour of his 'engaged' rival. She married the forester, while he continued to nurse his unhappy love and brood on his supposed rejection. Why? Did he, in the end, recoil from the domestic prospect, the humdrum life of marriage to a provincial girl? It was the period of Byronic romanticism; of flowing locks and the melancholy poetry of unrequited love. Perhaps these were the romantic emotions which underlay Andersen's strange behaviour in this case. Whatever the explanation, his renunciation was hardly

(*Right*) Andersen's pouch and the note about it by Jonas Collin the younger: 'This leather pouch was found after H. C. Andersen's death next to his breast. It contained a long letter from the loved one of his youth, Riborg Voigt. I burned the letter without reading it. J. Collin.'

(*Below*) Two drawings done by Andersen at about the time of the affair with Riborg Voigt. The mock-serious verse on the poet's tomb reads: 'Our little poet is no more, but we have what he created; he wrote and wrote – as others do. We know what we have lost!'

Riborg Voigt with her children

(*Below*) Bunch of flowers given to Riborg by Andersen

the end of the affair for either of them. After they had met again twelve years later, Anderson wrote the bitter-sweet fairy tale 'Sweethearts', in which, rationalizing, as he often did in his tales, he projects himself as the glad, independent spinning-top and Riborg as the ball that has lain sodden in the roof-gutter. But when he died in old age a pouch round his neck was found to contain a letter from her. She, in turn, kept some flowers that he gave to her. In accordance with his last wishes, the letter was destroyed unread. The pouch and the withered flowers are in the museum at Odense.

The unhappy love affair and some academic criticism of his work, which a less hypersensitive nature would have dismissed as trivial (though, after the initial setback, Andersen with devastating wit always gave more than he got), induced a period of deep despondency that was typical of him. The fatherly Collin urged

37

Adelbert von Chamisso   Ludwig Tieck

him to find relief in travel. And so, in the following spring, 1831,
he went abroad for the first time, to northern and central Germany.
He was away for about five weeks, meeting, at Dresden, Ludvig
Tieck, poet, author of fairy tales and translator of Shakespeare, and,
in Berlin, Adelbert von Chamisso, who was to be Andersen's first
German translator, and whose own *Peter Schlemihl* would later
suggest the theme of his blackest fairy tale, 'The Shadow'.

As always later, new impressions and acquaintances, especially
when the latter were famous or influential and able to further his
cause, soon restored his spirits. Home again, he wrote at top speed
the first of his vivid travel books, *Shadow Pictures of a Journey to the
Harz Mountains and Saxony*. It was published in September of the
same year. A wayward collection of stories, travel descriptions and
poems, loosely strung together, it was clearly inspired by Heinrich
Heine's *Reisebilder*, 1826–27.

Although he could always rely on the hospitality of patrons, and
indeed dined regularly with one or two of them, Andersen was
now having to earn his own living, since the public grant had run
out. Probably he could have got this extended, had he wanted to

attend the University, but that had never been his intention. Moreover, to the extent that his means would allow he was helping to
maintain his mother, who, widowed for the second time, had taken
to drink and was making growing demands on him. Financial
pressure, in addition to the unhappy affair with Riborg Voigt, may
partly explain the period of frantic over-production which followed
the visit to Germany, though probably there were more compulsive
reasons besides.

He had published a volume of poetry shortly before the *Shadow
Pictures*, and another appeared later in the same year. He wrote
a vaudeville which reached production. The next year, 1832, saw
the production of two operas to his librettos (one of them based on
Scott's *The Bride of Lammermoor*) and the rejection of a third (based
on *Kenilworth*, and produced after revision three years later). Yet
another collection of poems came out in the same year. In 1833 he
published his *Collected Poems*. He also adapted two plays from the
French and wrote two more vaudevilles, both of which were
rejected. Few of these latter works had much merit; and Andersen

Figure from *The Raven*, Andersen's
fairy opera (with J. P. E. Hartmann),
1832

(*Left*) From Andersen's diary of his
first journey abroad

only made things more difficult for himself by his emotional over-reaction to criticism. Furthermore, his undoubted peculiarities, of manner and appearance, and the obsessive desire to read his latest works to anyone who could be found to listen, rendered him in smart circles a figure of fun; to egg him on and then laugh at him behind his back soon became a fashionable parlour game. His friends, at first tactfully, later more insistently, tried with scant success to make him realize this.

Among his most dedicated friends, then as always, were the Collins. Jonas Collin, the senior government servant and close adviser of the absolutist king, had been Andersen's most influential patron. Among the first in Copenhagen to give the raw lad a helping hand, he had not only arranged for him to be educated but had supplied him in every crisis with fatherly advice and guidance. In time, he had virtually adopted him. For most of his adult life, Hans Christian Andersen lodged alone in furnished rooms, some-times at hotels; but Collin's house was always open to him, he dined there regularly, and in time he came to be regarded as one of the family. He often called it his 'home of homes'. Probably Jonas Collin, like almost everyone else, did not at first recognize, and possibly never fully recognized, the literary genius in Andersen; most likely, in the first place he had hoped, through a liberal educa-tion and personal help and encouragement, to train the talented youth for a profession or the civil service. But, whatever the initial responses, Collin's long, devoted and fatherly solicitude for Ander-sen's welfare, sometimes in trying circumstances, must be counted among the greatest in literary patronage.

Collin's second and most intelligent son, Edvard, Hans Christian's junior by three years, responded loyally to his father's suggestion that he should help to look after Andersen. Shrewd, well-balanced, level-headed and unemotional, legally trained, possibly a little unimaginative, he differed greatly in personality from the mercurial, emotional Andersen, but they became life-long friends, though they had their disagreements, complicated in character, and it was not in Edvard's nature to respond with the same fervency as Andersen. Edvard's good business head was a valuable asset in negotiations with publishers, and in seeing his friend's works through the press he was able to correct errors of spelling and punctuation. For it is a curious fact that, although he had gained a good academic examination, Andersen never man-aged to master the art of spelling. He would probably be diagnosed now as a case of dyslexia, or word-blindness, a condition un-related to intelligence quotients or, it would seem, literary ability.

The equable Collins must often have found their adoptive brother – who was temperamental, quick to take offence and liable at any

The Collins' house in Copenhagen

(*Below*) Andersen: a self-caricature

moment to burst into tears – a little trying, but they warmed to his naïve eagerness and his effervescent wit and humour. Some of them could not resist teasing him, and all of them, as he himself after-wards complained, were apt to 'educate' him; that is, to correct his various quirks and oddities and try to argue common sense into him. As always, he had the last word. In that famous piece of fictionalized autobiography, 'The Ugly Duckling', told, as the critic Georg Brandes said, in fewer words but with greater art than Andersen's official autobiography, we seem to hear the authentic Collin accents when the worldly-wise hen and cat urge the dis-contented duckling to stop moping and lay some eggs, or purr and make sparks fly.

There was one who never seemed to tease him, and who usually took his part and listened sympathetically to his complaints – the younger daughter, Louise. When, upset by some real or imagined slight, Andersen would rise from the table and rush weeping from

41

(*Right*) Henriette, wife of Jonas Collin

(*Below*) The Collins' house from the
street

(*Opposite*) Edvard Collin and his wife,
Henriette

The Swineherd; original illustration by Vilhelm Pedersen

the room, Louise would run out to comfort him and lead him back again. She had been no more than a child when Andersen had first visited the house, and he had drawn for her and told her stories and made paper dolls. They got on famously together.

When the affair with Riborg Voigt came to its apparent end, Andersen turned naturally for consolation to his old comforter, Louise. At nineteen, she was tall, blonde and blue-eyed; and while not conventionally pretty, was full of charm, warm-hearted and intelligent. He sent her a poem, flatteringly contrasting the 'celestial' blue of her eyes with the 'earthly' brown of Riborg's. Its tone was gay and light-hearted, and she did not take it very seriously. He then gave her his first draft autobiography to read. (More candid than the two which he afterwards published, and not intended for publication until after his death, it was discovered among his papers as late as 1925.)

She did not respond. But when his letters, though guarded, became increasingly ardent, she began to wonder if she had gone too far in her expressions of sympathy. She consulted her elder sister, the down-to-earth Ingeborg, who shrewdly advised her to let Andersen know that she was showing her their letters. Louise also took care never to be alone with him. This strategy had the intended inhibiting effect, and it is doubtful whether Andersen ever got as far as an explicit declaration of love. In fact, Louise was already in love with someone else, and the engagement was announced soon after. This time Andersen's suit had been hopeless from the start. Fairly or unfairly, Louise Collin appears in a number of the tales, 'The Swineherd' among others, as the haughty princess. In 'The Little Mermaid' she is the prince, Andersen himself the mermaid.

Andersen had come to a new crisis in his career. His emotional life was shattered and confused. In his writing he seemed to have reached a dead end. He had passed the peak, the critics agreed; he had 'culminated'. At this point, the Collins, Jonas and Edvard, suggested a course of treatment that had proved salutary before, and would do so from time to time in the future: they advised travel. What is more, they procured the means; they got him a public travel grant.

So in April 1833, to a great send-off by the assembled Collins, including Louise, Andersen, now aged twenty-eight, took ship for Germany on a journey that was to last fifteen months, with Italy as the ultimate destination. Travelling along the Rhine, which was disappointing (the songs and the wine were the best things about it, he thought), he proceeded to Paris, stayed there a month, and went on, via Switzerland, to Milan, Genoa and Florence, arriving in Rome in mid-October. There, with intervening visits to Naples, Capri, Pompeii, Amalfi and Paestum, he lingered for six months,

(*Opposite*) Louise Collin

44

Andersen kept a record of his foreign travels in diaries and many drawings. The sketches on this and the next page, from his first journey in Italy, show: the Tiber at Rome, the Greek temples at Paestum, Amalfi and the Ponte Vecchio in Florence

seeing all the sights, soaking in the atmosphere and spending his evenings in the convivial company of the Scandinavian writers and artists, presided over by the sculptor, and grand old man, Thorvaldsen, who had settled in the Italian capital. (They foregathered at the Caffè Greco, the famous establishment in the Via Condotti, which was the haunt, at various times, of many foreign artists and writers, among them Casanova, Goethe, Gogol, Byron and Liszt.) Before leaving for home via Salzburg and Munich, he also visited Bologna, Ferrara, Padua and Venice.

While in Switzerland, he had completed a romantic drama in verse, *Agnete and the Merman*, based on an old Danish ballad. It was to be his *magnum opus* and, full of the highest hopes, he sent it home to Edvard Collin for publication. Edvard was severely critical; to Andersen's great distress, as his diaries reveal. But he dutifully transcribed it and saw it through the press. His judgment had been sound: a few good lyrics apart, it was a misbegotten piece, and was savaged by the critics. Now Andersen *was* finished, they said. Word of the fiasco reached him in Rome, where he received the further bad news that his mother had died in an Odense home. He was plunged into the deepest despair.

Far from being finished, however, Hans Christian Andersen was just about to begin. It is characteristic of this extraordinarily resilient man that he never, even in his blackest moods, admitted

Florence 12 April 1834.

Opposite:
(*Left*) Bertel Thorvaldsen (1768–1844)

(*Right*) Andersen, painted in Rome

(*Below*) The Caffè Greco, Rome, in 1842

(*Above*) Andersen's drawing of the Spanish Steps in Rome

Thorvaldsen's house in the Via Sistina, by Andersen

defeat – at least not for long – but always fought back again. One of the critics had called him an improviser, implying that he was shallow, and that he was incapable of sustained thought or construction. Very well; this was an idea.

The public art of composing impromptu verses on subjects suggested by the audience, Italian in origin, was still practised in Italy; Andersen had seen several such performances. He decided that he would write a novel, in which he, the improviser, would be the hero.

He started on the work almost at once, while he was still in Rome, and he finished it soon after his return to Copenhagen. *The Improvisatore* is Andersen's own story, as it had been and would be, set in Italy. The poor boy Antonio, the improvising poet of the market place, who succeeds in the face of every criticism and eventually becomes famous, is Andersen himself. This was what he had always said he would do: 'First you go through a cruel time and then you become famous,' he had told his mother. She, too, was in the book, as also were his friends and enemies: the Collins, the Meislings, brilliantly caricatured, and the critics, chief among these being an academic Professor Habbas Dahdah, whose name apparently derives from Danish dog-Latin, *habeas da-da* – or 'I'll give him what's what'.

Twenty-five years before, Madame de Staël had written a similar autobiographical work, set in Italy, *Corinne, ou l'Italie* (1807), that is regarded as her fictional masterpiece. Andersen knew this novel in translation, and almost certainly took it as his model. *The Improvisatore*, however, is a better book, the autobiographical story and the Italian setting more successfully integrated. While in its factual descriptions of scenery and architecture, *Corinne*, in parts, reads like Baedeker, *The Improvisatore* presents a splendidly exciting picture of Italy in the early nineteenth century. It is the Italy of the romantic movement; but, remembering his own impoverished childhood, Andersen is aware of the poverty and disease which lurk behind the colour and the beauty. The book's weaknesses are Andersen's failure to develop his characters satisfactorily, and its melodramatic ending. These faults were to flaw his subsequent novels, none of which attains to the level of *The Improvisatore*.

Published in April 1835, a week after its author's thirtieth birthday, and dedicated 'in filial and fraternal affection' to the Collins, it was an immediate success. A German translation, appearing a year later, established Andersen at one stroke as a major international writer. The book was also a success in England when Richard Bentley published it, in Mary Howitt's translation from the German, in 1845. It was the first of Andersen's works to be translated into English. Its influence was widespread; in Denmark

Drawing by Andersen of the view from his window in Nyhavn, Copenhagen

(*Below*) Nyhavn, the canal-side street in Copenhagen where Andersen occupied rooms at various times, first in the middle house in the picture and finally in the taller building on the right

Little Claus and Big Claus; original illustration by Vilhelm Pedersen

itself, it probably inspired one of the central works in the romantic ballet, Bournonville's *Napoli*.

While *The Improvisatore* was going through the press, Andersen turned to other ideas. Writing to a friend in February 1835, he said: 'I have started on some "Tales told for Children", and seem to be making good progress with them. I have done a couple of the stories I remember having liked when little, and that I think are not generally known. I have written them exactly as I would tell them to a child.'

The tiny volume of sixty-four small pages, badly printed on poor paper, which appeared on 8 May 1835, a month after *The Improvisatore*, contained 'The Tinder Box', 'Little Claus and Big Claus', 'The Princess on the Pea' and 'Little Ida's Flowers'.

It had a bad reception. In the opinion of one influential critic, while such tales might do very well for adults, they were quite unsuitable for children. It was true that children might find them amusing, but where was the instruction? It was a strange 'dream' for a princess to go riding on a dog's back, at night, to a soldier's lodgings, and be kissed by him. There was more immorality in the

(*Opposite*) Andersen in 1836; from a painting by C. A. Jensen

Hans Christian Ørsted (1777–1851), physicist

tale about the parish clerk who visits the farmer's wife while her husband is away, and which tells how she pours wine for him, while he 'speared' the fish, 'because he was very fond of fish'. What sort of language was this? As for the story of Big Claus clubbing Little Claus's grandmother to death, and then Little Claus clubbing *him*, as if they had been oxen, was this sort of violence likely to inspire respect for human life? The tale about the princess on the pea, besides implying that ladies of rank were always so thin-skinned, could have other harmful effects. The style also was condemned; for it offended against the rigid academic conventions, and, deliberately, as Andersen had said, aimed at being colloquial. 'Conceive what Johnson and Burke would have thought of *Alice in Wonderland*,' Edmund Gosse, who met Andersen, said, 'and you have a parallel to the effect of "Little Claus and Big Claus" upon academic Denmark.' In the light of this early criticism of the fairy

54

tales, it is strange to think that they should now, in England and America, be so often dismissed as suitable only for the nursery.

Not all the critics were as obtuse as the one who has been quoted, but most of them agreed in adjuring Andersen to stop wasting his time on such unworthy material. Even the most generous of them, on the whole, preferred the novel, as indeed Andersen did himself. The most perceptive of those few who thought otherwise was neither a critic nor, primarily, a literary man. He was H. C. Ørsted, the discoverer of electro-magnetism, who is commemorated in the international term for a unit of magnetic intensity – an oersted. He had been one of Andersen's first and most loyal patrons, and a lasting friendship had developed between the two. In a letter to another friend, written before either *The Improvisatore* or the first of the fairy tales had been published, Andersen said: 'Ørsted says that if *The Improvisatore* makes me famous, the fairy tales will make me immortal; they are the most perfect things I have written. But I don't think so.' Ørsted also saw further than most of his contemporaries when he declared that Andersen was 'greatest in the humorous'. While it would probably be safe to say that the prime attractions of the fairy tales to Victorian readers were their romantic, sentimental and melodramatic features, what mainly appeals to a modern reader is their great wit and humour, though this is often obscured in the poor Victorian translations that are still current.

Andersen was already at work on a second novel, *O.T.*, and this was published in the following year, 1836. Like the first, it is transparently autobiographical, but, unlike that, it is set in contemporary Denmark. The initials stand both for the hero, Otto Thostrup, who is Andersen, and Odense Gaol (Odense Tugthus), where Thostrup was born. The letters have been branded on Thostrup's shoulder in childhood by his evil genius, a blackmailing gipsy who appears at intervals to remind him of his miserable birth, and to insinuate that a certain deformed and depraved character is, wrongly as it turns out, his twin sister. The allusions to Andersen's own early environment and dubious half-sister are obvious. So also is the meaning of the interwoven story of Thostrup's efforts to assert his equality with the assured and unemotional friend, Baron Vilhelm, who represents Edvard Collin. The book is sentimental, and of its period typically melodramatic, with gipsies and other romantic apparatus derived from Scott. It is mainly of interest today as a *roman à clef*, and for its well-sketched period background, which caused it and Andersen's third novel to be sub-titled 'Life in Denmark', echoing the sub-title 'Life in Italy' of *The Improvisatore*, when they were published together in English translation in 1845, the same year as the first.

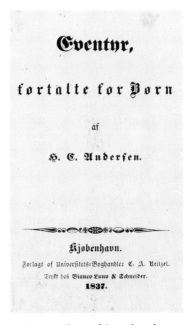

Title-page of one of the early volumes of fairy tales, given by the author to Mathilde Ørsted

The third novel, *Only a Fiddler*, which appeared a year later, in 1837, is yet another variation on the theme of Andersen. But in this case the poor boy, Christian, although he develops into a great violinist, ultimately fails through ill luck and want of appreciation, and dies a village fiddler and a pauper. Like its predecessor, *Only a Fiddler* is full of fine descriptive passages, but once again Andersen fails to master the full-length medium; as a novel, it is episodic like the others, and falls apart in the end.

The implications about the tragic consequences of failure to recognize and reward genius should have been obvious to the critics, but mostly they reacted against the book's sentimentalism and self-pity. One of the sternest critics was the philosopher Kierkegaard, who devoted a large part of his first book, *From the Papers of One Still Living*, to castigating the novel and its author, whom he called a 'sniveller'. The effect on Andersen, wont to react over-sensitively to even the mildest of slights, was shattering. As always, he responded with some barbed comments later on. Alluding to the clotted Hegelian style of this debut work, in his autobiography *The Fairy Tale of My Life* (1855), he recorded an alleged joke to the effect that only Kierkegaard and Andersen himself had ever read the book through; and in a later novel, *To Be or Not To Be* (1857), he makes one of the characters say that she was 'tired of crawling over the style's pavement to get at the temple of thought; the road was so long, and the greenery she found there not so freshly sprung.' That Kierkegaard's attack still rankled a quarter of a century later is clear from the caustic little parable 'The Snail and the Rose Bush' (1861), in which the snail (Kierkegaard) spits at the world and retires into its shell, while the rose (Andersen) keeps on blooming, because it 'can do no other'.

After *Only a Fiddler*, Andersen turned from the novel to make a determined assault on his first love, the theatre. Since his initial attempts at play-writing, a few minor works had been produced, including a couple of operas drawn from Scott and a third from an original by Carlo Gozzi. One or two of these had even been moderately successful. Now, in 1838, he embarked upon his first major stage play, a romantic drama in verse, *The Mulatto*, which reached production in February 1840. Based on a French story by Madame Reybaud, and set in Martinique in the eighteenth century, it is about a sensitive mulatto who, after many tribulations, marries his beloved, a white countess. Needless to say, the eponymous hero and social outcast is yet another self-projection, the countess being probably an idealization of Louise Collin. The public took to the play – with its 'novel effects' which included a slave market – and it achieved a successful run of twenty-one performances. The critical reception, however, was rather mixed, some of the reviewers attack-

Søren Kierkegaard, *c.* 1840

Nye Eventyr.

Andersen's inscription in a copy of *New Fairy Tales*: 'Dear Hr Kierkegaard! *Either* (whether) you like my little ones *Or* you do not like them, they come without *Fear and Trembling* and that at any rate is something. Yours most sincerely, The author.' *Either Or* and *Fear and Trembling* are titles of works by Kierkegaard

ing it, unreasonably, as an adaptation, implying that it was unoriginal.

Andersen's reaction to the criticism was to write an entirely original play, *The Moorish Maid*, a melodrama with a Spanish setting. *The Mulatto* had owed some of its success to the leading performer, Johanne Luise Heiberg, who was the greatest Danish actress of the century. She turned down the name part in *The Moorish Maid*, however, and the play also ran into difficulties with the theatre's new director, her husband Johan Ludvig Heiberg, the doyen of Danish letters, and the critic who had called Andersen an improviser. Andersen had gone off on his next, extensive journey abroad when the play eventually reached the stage. It ran for only three unsuccessful performances. The failure induced in him the same deep misery as earlier setbacks, and worse was to follow. In Heiberg's satirical play, *A Soul after Death*, which also appeared while Andersen was abroad, the damned in hell have to endure the double torment of witnessing *The Mulatto* and *The Moorish Maid* on a single evening. Andersen's own torments after this can be imagined; but the riposte came, as always, in due course. In *A Poet's Bazaar* (1842), he tells how, in a dream, he, too, descends to hell, where, true enough, he finds his plays being given exactly as related by Heiberg. He learns also that it had been the intention to conclude with a play by Heiberg – *Fata Morgana*, another failure – but that the damned had objected that even hell could be too hot and there should be moderation in all things. It is worth recording that the passage was written after returning from a dinner given in honour of Heiberg by the Collins: although Andersen went home early, at least the two men were on speaking terms.

A Poet's Bazaar, the best of Andersen's lively travel books, was the fruit of a journey, lasting nine months, to Italy, Greece and Turkey. The circumstances that inspired the journey were characteristic. There was Mrs Heiberg's refusal to play the lead in *The Moorish Maid*, to which Andersen had reacted petulantly; there was a nagging premonition that the play would not succeed, and that he would meet with a further barrage of criticism; and, finally, there was the approaching wedding of Louise Collin, which had at last been fixed after a long engagement. 'The south is my bride,' he exclaimed. Foreign travel had before provided both balm and inspiration. It was time to try the remedy again. 'To travel is to live,' he wrote to a friend. 'Then life becomes rich and vivid, and you don't, like the pelican, live on your own blood.' He now had the money to travel. He had not done too badly out of *The Mulatto*, and he had been granted a small state pension. 'At last,' he said, 'I have a little breadfruit tree in my garden, and need no longer sing for crumbs.' During the course of his journey, old Collin wrote to inform him that he had been allotted an additional travel bursary.

Leaving Copenhagen on the last day of October 1841, he went via Munich and Rome to Naples, from there by ship to Piraeus, calling at Malta, and then, after spending a month in Athens, on to Smyrna and Constantinople, across the Black Sea to Constantsa, in what is now Rumania, up the Danube to Budapest and Vienna, and so home again. It was an adventurous and, in its middle stages, a rather hazardous journey. Few western travellers ventured behind the silken curtain of Turkish-controlled Europe. Besides all the uncertainties and likely discomforts and inconveniences of Oriental life, the plagues and problematic sanitation, there were the irksome formalities of quarantine; for example, ten days of close confinement on the Austrian-Turkish frontier at Orsava, by the Iron Gate. Although Greece had regained her independence twenty years before, the Slavs along the Danube were in revolt, with fighting going on in some areas. It cost the pusillanimous Andersen a sleepless night in Constantinople before he decided to reject the cautious

(*Opposite*) Vesuvius from Naples; drawing by Andersen

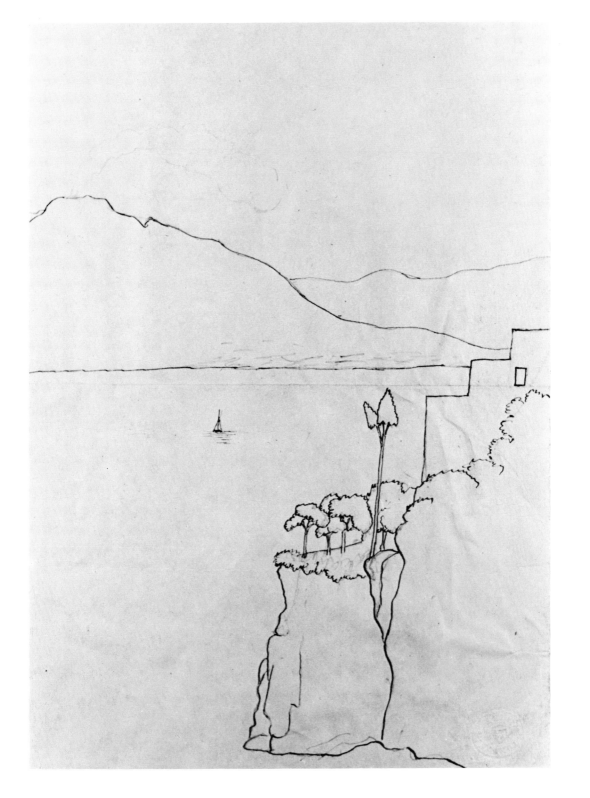

(*Above*) Carlsplatz in Munich, drawn by Andersen

Andersen, before 1833

advice of nearly everyone to return home through Greece the way he had come.

For a man of Andersen's nature this seems an astonishing decision, as indeed the whole journey is astonishing. Yet it was also typical of him. A war of nerves was always going on in Hans Christian Andersen, between the thrust of ambition and determination to succeed whatever the cost on the one hand, and, on the other, his extreme timidity and hypersensitiveness. His deep-seated urge to travel and the often comically grotesque fears connected with travelling exemplify it. Probably in the nineteenth century it was wise to beware of dogs in strange places, in view of rabies; but Andersen had a manic dread of even the most innocent-looking animals, and he seems never to have eaten pork, from fear of trichinosis. He would arrive at the station hours before his train was due to depart, would be sure when it started that he had taken the wrong one, and would suffer further agonies as he rummaged for his passport, convinced that he had forgotten it. His luggage included a coil of rope in case of fire at his hotel. Leaving his room, he would turn back twice to make sure that the candles were out,

(*Left*) Andersen's Turkish passport

A camel at the Acropolis; drawing by Andersen

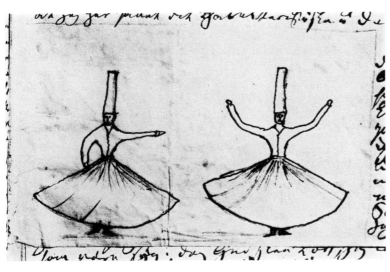

Dancing dervishes at Pera, Constantinople, by Andersen

and still be uncertain when he got into the street. It is plausibly related that he used to leave a note by his bedside, 'I only seem dead', afraid of being buried alive. Yet when it came to the crunch the compulsive traveller was ready to face almost any hazard that came, if not always with a cheer, certainly with his eyes open.

A Poet's Bazaar is an enchanting book – as the title suggests, a vivid, crowded, shifting pattern of colourful people and places, an Oriental kaleidoscope. Witty, amusing, poetic, sharp and precise in its descriptions of scenery, moods and atmosphere, and free from the sentimentalism and self-pity of the novels, it is, alongside *The Improvisatore,* the best of Andersen's full-length works. Development of character and the construction of plot, essential to the novel in the nineteenth century, were beyond his powers; the travel book, relaxed in form and style, suited him. Although his critics, still applying their academic yardsticks, were largely blind to its merits, it was a popular success at home and it added to its author's growing fame abroad.

Some of Andersen's belongings, including trunks, hatbox, umbrella and coil of rope

Caricature, 1863, of Andersen and a chestnut-seller in Spain

Other travel books would follow: *In Sweden, 1851*; *In Spain, 1863*; and *A Visit to Portugal, 1866, 1868*. Andersen was to remain an untiring tourist almost to the end. He travelled by every available means: on foot, by steamer and sailing ship, by stage coach and hired carriage, on horseback and on mules, later increasingly by train. Rail travel, then in its infancy, fascinated him, as the 'romance' of travel by coach did not. He knew its discomforts: up at dawn, the long wait in the cold, the snail's pace, the jolting tightly-packed vehicle, the rubbing shoulders with chattering, egotistical fellow-travellers. There is a delicious account of an insufferable English companion in *A Poet's Bazaar*, told with malicious wit: thus, as Andersen said in another connection, he 'got his money back'. By contrast, trains were fast and comfortable, and he could sit and watch the world go by, as he rarely could in a coach, with its obstructed view.

The railway, he believed, would have a beneficial effect in bringing people together, and after railways would come air travel. In a prophetic little sketch, 'In Thousands of Years' Time' (1852) – it was to come true sooner than he imagined – he predicted that

63

The Emperor's New Clothes; illustration
by Vilhelm Pedersen

'young Americans' would 'come flying on wings of steam' to see
'our ancient monuments and crumbling ruins'. '"There's a lot to
see in Europe," said the young American, "and we saw it in a week.
It's quite possible to do this, as the great traveller" (mentioning
a contemporary name) "has shown in his celebrated work, *Europe
Seen in Eight Days*."' The tale anticipates Jules Verne, who must
surely have read it when he wrote *Around the World in Eighty Days*,
twenty years later. Andersen's lively interest in scientific development, owing a good deal to his friendship with Ørsted, also
included wireless telegraphy. Humorously, he speculated on the
possibility, at some future date, of listening in Copenhagen to his
friend Liszt playing the piano in Weimar.

In spite of the generally unfavourable reception given to his first
four fairy tales in May 1835, and his own failure as yet to realize that
in them he had found his proper medium, he had published three
more tales later in the same year. None had appeared the next year,
but a third little volume, which included two of his best-known
tales, 'The Little Mermaid' and 'The Emperor's New Clothes',
came out in 1837, and from then on he invariably published a new
volume each Christmas. Of the first four tales, only the inferior
'Little Ida's Flowers' had been 'original', and even this one had
borrowed from a tale by E. T. A. Hoffmann. The others, like some
of the later tales, were retellings of stories Andersen had heard as
a child in the spinning room and during hop-picking, together
with reminiscences of others, such as the Aladdin story in *A Thousand and One Nights*, which is the basis of the very first fairy tale,
'The Tinder Box'. However, Andersen's individual accent can be

heard in all these tales from the start: in the ironic aside, the thumb-nail caricature and the satire in miniature, in the employment of concrete imagery, in the economy of the style, and in the colloquial ease which so offended the first, academic critics.

Edvard Collin has left an excellent account of the genesis of Andersen's tales, which were always told or read aloud before being printed.

He did not say [Collin wrote], 'The children got into the carriage and they drove off'; but 'Then they got into the carriage. Goodbye, Daddy! Goodbye, Mummy! The whip cracked, snick-snack; and off they went: gee-up, come on there!'

It is in just this way that 'The Tinder Box' starts off: not with 'Once upon a time', but: 'A soldier came marching along the high

Vilhelm Pedersen's illustration of
The Little Mermaid

road: Left, right! Left, right!' And it ends, not with the traditional 'and they lived happily ever after', but: 'The wedding feast lasted a week, and the dogs sat up at table with the rest and were all eyes.' To quote Andersen in his own notes to the collected edition, 1862: 'The voice of the narrator had to be heard in the style, which therefore had to approach the spoken word. The stories were told for children, but the adult had to be able to listen to them.' This latter point may not fully express Andersen's original intentions, but it is what happened, and as time went on the tales were written mainly or wholly for the adult.

Even in these early tales there are many passages that are appreciated by the mature reader and are not fully understood by children; such as the ironical references to the soldier's changing fortunes in 'The Tinder Box':

He was rich and well-dressed now and had lots of friends, who all said he was a fine fellow and a perfect gentleman. . . . But as he was spending money every day and never getting any back again, he found himself in the end with only two ha'pennies left. And so he had to move out of the grand rooms he had been living in and go into a tiny little attic under the roof, where he had to clean his own boots. . . . And none of his friends came to see him, because there were so many stairs to climb.

Or the scene in 'Little Claus and Big Claus' where Little Claus happens to eavesdrop on the farmer's wife while she is entertaining her lover, the parish clerk:

He was such a good husband, but he had one failing: he couldn't bear the sight of parish clerks. If a parish clerk showed his face he would get quite angry. That was why the clerk had called on the woman when he knew her husband was away, and why the good wife had put before him all her nicest food.

As Andersen said later, as regards his original conscious intentions again, perhaps, protesting too much: 'I get an idea for grown-ups and then tell my tale to the little ones, while remembering that Mother and Father will be listening and must have something to think about.' Incidentally, he toned down the first draft of 'Little Claus and Big Claus', substituting a parish clerk for the original parson. Some of his translators have gone further in discretion by making him a farm bailiff or, in one wild case, the woman's brother, thus, of course, making a hash of the whole erotic point.

Translators have plodded heavily through Andersen's subtleties, and at the same time they, or their editors, contending perhaps with poor texts, have altered, adapted and bowdlerized beyond all rhyme or reason. Some early versions were re-translations from German; some betray an inadequate knowledge of Danish, and others, produced by Scandinavians, inadequate command of English. The over-all result, in very many cases, has been to rub off the literary qualities of these highly wrought tales – their colloquial ease, the economy, the subtle idioms and ironies, the alliterations,

Title-page of the first German edition
of the fairy tales, 1839

the prose rhythms and prose poetry – so reducing Andersen to the lowest nursery level and making his works a cheap quarry to be raided for every new twopence-coloured edition. Andersen is extremely difficult to translate, ultimately perhaps impossible to translate adequately, but the job could have been done better than it has been. Take, for example, that little masterpiece, only 1,500 words long, 'The Princess on the Pea'.

(*Overleaf*) Andersen's tales turned into strip cartoons: *The Princess on the Pea* (Danish) and *The Steadfast Tin Soldier* (German)

Kongedatteren paa Erten.

Der var en Gang en Prinds som vilde gifte sig, men det skulde være en rigtig Kongedatter som han vilde have.

Nu reiste han igjennem hele Verden for at finde denne men over alt havde han noget at dadle.

Ingensteds fandt han hvad han søgte.

Prindsesinder gaves der nok, men om de vare virkelige Kongedøttre kunde han ikke saae at vide.

Alle Tider var der Noget som ikke var ganske rigtig.

Da gik han hjem igjen, og var ganske bedrøvet at han ikke kunde finde en virkelig Kongedatter.

Een Aften var der et frygtelig Uveir det lynede, tordnede og regnede.

Da bankede det om Natten paa Tøren.

Den gamle Konge gik selv ned for at lukke Tøren op.

Det var en Kongedatter som stod for Tøren. Herre Gud! hvor saae hun ud.

Det gamle Kongepar tænkte nu vil vi dog see om det er en rigtig Kongedatter.

Den gamle Dronning gik selv ind i Sovekamret, tog alle Dyner og Matrater ud af Sengen og lagde en liden Erte paa Bunden.

Nu tog hun 20 Matratzer og lagde paa Erten, og saa endnu 20 Dyner ovenpaa.

Den anden Dags Morgen spurgte Kongedatteren over at hun ikke have kunnet sove, for di hun havde lagt paa Noget haardt.

Nu kunde de see at det var en virkelig Kongedatter og Prindsen tog hende til sin Gemalinde.

Men Erten kom paa Kunstkammeret hvor man kan saae den at see, naar man ikke er stjaalet.

Druck und Verlag von Oehmigke & Riemschneider in Neu Ruppin.   N 3056

Der standhafte Zinnsoldat.

Oehmigke & Riemschneider in Neu-Ruppin.

No. 3429.

'Αμέσως τότε ἐκατάλαβαν ὅτι ἦτο τῷ ὄντι ἀληθινὴ βασιλοπούλα, ἀφοῦ μέσα ἀπὸ εἴκοσι στρώματα
καὶ εἴκοσι παπλώματα τὴν ἐπόνεσε τὸ ρεβίθι. Μόνον
μία ἀληθινὴ βασιλοπούλα ἠμποροῦσε νὰ εἶναι τόσον
εὐαίσθητη!

Λοιπὸν τὴν ὑπάνδρευσαν μὲ τὸν υἱὸν τοῦ βα-
σιλέως, ἀφοῦ ἐκατάλαβαν ὅτι ἦτο ἀληθινὴ βασι-

The Princess on the Pea; from a Greek
edition (illustration after Vilhelm
Pedersen)

Thumbelina, from a German edition

14

Ein niedlicher, weißer Schmetterling umflatterte sie stets und
ließ sich zuletzt auf das Blatt nieder, denn Däumelinchen gefiel
ihm. Diese war sehr erfreut; denn nun konnte die Kröte sie nicht
erreichen, und es war so schön, wo sie fuhr; die Sonne schien
auf das Wasser, dieses glänzte wie das herrlichste Gold. Sie
nahm ihren Gürtel, band das Ende um den Schmetterling, das
andere Ende des Bandes befestigte sie am Blatte; das glitt nun
viel schneller davon und sie mit, denn sie stand ja auf demselben.

Wie war das arme Däumelinchen erschroken, als der Maikäfer
mit ihr auf den Baum flog! Aber hauptsächlich war sie des schönen,
weißen Schmetterlinges wegen betrübt, den sie an das Blatt fest-

Prudish translators, or their editors, have shied at the title, and renamed the tale 'The Princess and the Pea' or 'The Real Princess'. The alteration is unimportant, but unnecessary. Worse is the substitution of 'bean' for 'pea', presumably for the same puritanical reason that the 'cock' in another tale is called, in America, the 'rooster', and 'stones' are 'rocks'. Some versions have three peas instead of one: there is safety – but can also be superfluity – in numbers. The tale plays delightfully throughout on the word 'real(ly)', but instead of this deliberate repetition we are given elegant variations, with frequent use of the word 'proper'. The rhythms pass unregarded. Idioms are translated literally. Danish, more logical in this case than English, has 'lightened and thundered', and so the phrase comes over in some of the translations. (There are many far worse examples of literalness in other tales.) Andersen's story ends simply: 'Now that was a real story!' But in an unusually well illustrated English edition, one that is recommended in handbooks as the best, this is replaced by: 'Was not this a lady of real delicacy?' Little wonder that people with any real literary sensibility often speak contemptuously of Andersen, when this is the substitute they have been brought up on.

The disastrous catalogue would fill a book. Clumsy circumlocutions abound where the original is economical; as at the end of 'The Tinder Box', where the dogs 'were all eyes' ('made big eyes') is spun out long-windedly. Calculated absurdities and banalities are 'rationalized' and flattened out. The banal emperor in 'The Swineherd', for example, is made to exclaim that the rose is 'more than pretty, it's beautiful', when what he says is: 'It's more than pretty, it's nice!' The lady in waiting in 'The Tinder Box' puts on seven-league boots in the translations, in order to run faster, where Andersen absurdly says 'waders' or 'water-boots'. He chose his words carefully, and if he had meant 'seven-league boots' he would have said so; he used the term in other tales.

In a pioneer study of the fairy tales a distinguished Danish scholar, Hans Brix, observed that the best of them were neither the products of an idle imagination nor were they invented merely in order to thrill or entertain. 'In every one of them', he wrote, 'there is a drop of the writer's heart's blood; and that is why they remain fresh and alive, while innumerable attempts to imitate them have failed.' Andersen himself said: 'Most of what I have written is a reflection of myself. Every character is from life. I know and have known them all.' Of his original tales he wrote, in the notes to the collected edition, that they lay in his mind like a grain of corn, needing only a current, a ray of sunshine or a drop of gall for them to unfold. A typical example of this generative process is provided by one of the most perfect of the fairy tales, 'The Nightingale'.

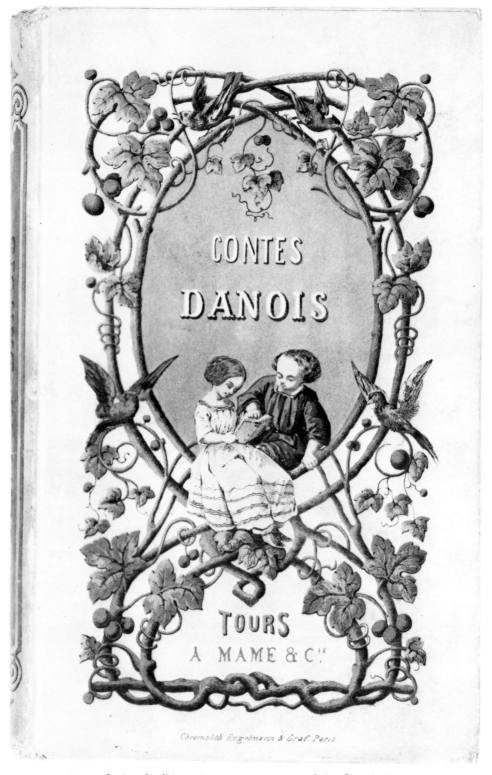

CONTES

DANOIS

TOURS

A MAME & C.ᴵᴱ

Chromolith Engelmann & Graf Paris

Cover of a French edition, 1853; an anonymous translation from the German

The Story of a Mother; from a Bengali edition

'The Nightingale' is an allegory, which sets up true poetry, the real nightingale, 'which has never been heard of at court', against academic literature, the mechanical nightingale, 'which always sang the same tune'. 'For you see. . . with the real nightingale you can never know what to expect. But with the artificial one everything is fixed. Just so, and in no other way. It can be explained!' And: 'It sang the same tune over and over thirty-three times, and never grew tired.' Consequently, the real nightingale was banished from the empire, while the mechanical one was honoured with a silken

72

cushion close to the emperor's bed and the title of High Imperial Bedside Table Singer, 'ranking number one on the left'. And the music-master wrote twenty-five volumes about it, 'long and learned, and full of the most difficult Chinese words; and everybody said they had read and understood them; for if they hadn't they would have been stupid and would have been punched in the stomach.' 'The emperor, the court and every other Chinaman knew each little cluck of the mechanical bird's song by heart, but that was just why they liked it best: they could join in the singing, as they did.' But then one day the mechanical nightingale went 'Zup!' as something snapped inside it. There was no more singing at court,

The Nightingale; illustrations by
Vilhelm Pedersen

and soon the emperor lay on his death-bed. But eventually he was revived by the return of the real nightingale; and 'The servants came in to see to their dead emperor and – well, there they stood, and the emperor said: "Good morning!"'

All this Andersen knew only too well; it had been a part of his own bitter experience. In this very way the pundits had preferred the stale literary conventions to his fresh 'native wood-notes wild'. Thus the nightingale is another self-projection. But, as in many other cases, the 'grain of corn' stored up in his mind had been waiting for a generating impulse, a 'ray of sunshine or drop of gall'. The activator here was Jenny Lind.

After the unhappy affairs with Riborg Voigt and Louise Collin, Andersen's susceptible heart had fluttered briefly for at least two others, both women a good deal younger than himself and both richer. The latter fact, among others, probably helped to restrain him; he always doubted his financial ability to maintain a wife and family, but would not have wanted to be kept by his wife. In any case, one of the women, Sophie Ørsted, the daughter of his scientist friend and patron, forestalled him by announcing her engagement to someone else. Now, however, he was to meet the grand passion of his middle years.

Although only twenty when they first met in 1840, Jenny Lind had already established herself as an operatic star in Stockholm, and a local journalist had called her 'The Swedish Nightingale', a name by which she would be known ever after. But, as yet, she was known to very few outside Sweden; one of the few even in Denmark who had heard her name was Andersen, who had travelled in Sweden the year before her first visit to Copenhagen. Seeing her name in the list of guests at the Copenhagen hotel where he happened to be staying between removals, he paid his respects to her, and learnt that she had crossed the Sound with her father for a few days of sightseeing in the Danish capital. The meeting was quite formal, and Andersen retained no great impression of the girl. But when she returned in order to give some guest performances in the autumn of 1843, three years later, on what was her first foreign tour, it was another story. Andersen's diary records its progress: 10 September, 'In love'; 18 September, 'I love her'. By this time they had been meeting daily, and when she left for home two days later he passed a letter to her, which, the diary records, 'she must understand'.

She did understand. Better than most, she understood the struggle he had had to endure. She had known poverty herself. She responded sympathetically to him as an artist. She herself had some of the same sensitivity; and she entered eagerly into his ebullient fun and gaiety. She always enjoyed his company, but she did not love

(*Opposite*) Jenny Lind

The Pantomime Theatre in the Tivoli
gardens, Copenhagen

him; and told him so in letters then and later. They met again two years after, at a celebration dinner given at her Copenhagen hotel on the eve of her departure. Sadly he wrote in his diary that night: 'She toasted me as her brother!' And the next day: 'Said goodbye to Jenny!'

They met later in the year in Berlin, where she was continuing her triumphal progress through Europe. Fully expecting an invitation from her for Christmas Eve, he declined every other invitation. But none came. He spent a miserable evening alone in his hotel. In answer to his complaints, the next morning, she teasingly remarked that she had supposed he would be in the company of 'princes and princesses'; but, to make good the loss, she invited him for New Year's Eve. The Christmas tree was hung with presents, all for him, and she sang for him an aria and some Swedish songs. It was a memorable evening. But she had been careful to invite a chaperon to share it with them. The story of the two 'geniuses of the North' meeting under the Christmas tree in the German capital got into the papers, and must have made melancholy reading for Andersen.

They met again at intervals, in London and at Weimar. But she persisted in calling him 'brother'. She was his last love. At forty, he seems finally to have resigned himself to lonely bachelorhood.

Jenny Lind, 'The Swedish Nightingale', triumphed with her natural song over the fashionable Italian opera-singers of her day,

76

just as Andersen had triumphed, or would triumph, over the academic *littérateurs*. 'The Nightingale' is thus both a literary allegory and a tribute to the woman Andersen admired and loved, and in part identified himself with. This many-faceted masterpiece also contains reminiscences of the Aladdin story that Andersen had been told by his father many years before in Odense, and of the *chinoiserie* of the Tivoli gardens, founded in Copenhagen in the year of the tale's publication, 1843. In addition, of course, to the 'trappings' every child understands and enjoys.

'The Nightingale' was published together with 'The Ugly Duckling', and with that and 'The Little Mermaid', published six years earlier, is among the best-known of Andersen's fairy tales.

The Ugly Duckling; illustration by
Vilhelm Pedersen

Charles Dickens

Neither of the latter stories is artistically its equal, both being flawed by false happy endings: as Brandes aptly observed, the duckling emerges as a domesticated instead of a wild swan; while the mermaid, in a basically sentimental tale which would hardly in any objective assessment be included among Andersen's greatest, ascends on rose-red clouds to an ultimate heaven its author never really believed in. Like so much in Andersen, his attitude to religion was highly complex: he talked much of a divinity that had shaped his ends, of a benevolent Father who had watched over him, so that everything had turned out for the best, but he was hardly ever a conventional believer and never a churchgoer. His religious philosophy seems to have been rather an amalgam of his father's rationalism and his mother's pagan superstition, with now one, now the other uppermost.

The immense popularity of 'The Little Mermaid' in Victorian times and later probably did a lot to establish Andersen's image among literary people as that of a writer of sentimental fairy tales and no more. Certainly he was sentimental; but so too was Dickens, his great contemporary – consider only Little Nell and the death of Paul Dombey. And both Andersen and Dickens could be theatrical and melodramatic; they were equally children of their time, and sentimentality and melodrama were in the air. But to dismiss Andersen as sentimental is as absurd as it would be to write off Dickens for the same reason; both are far greater than their faults. True, Andersen did not promote social reforms. He showed little interest in political affairs, and admitted his ignorance of them. *A Poet's Bazaar* says very little about the struggle then being waged to liberate eastern Europe from the Turks. He was not a political animal, and was in many respects a social climber. At the same time, he never concealed his lowly origins, and he spoke up time and again in his novels, plays and fairy tales for the poor and despised.

Andersen is a greater stylist than Dickens, though the assertion is difficult to sustain, in view of the impossibility of recapturing in another language a prose style so perfectly married to its medium, where the sentences seem now to trip and dance on the page, and now, in heightened passages, rise to the sheerest poetry. One can only try, thanklessly, to catch a little of the magic in sentences such as this, in 'The Nightingale':

And Death gave up each of his treasures for a song while the nightingale went on singing, singing of the silent churchyard where the white roses grow, where the elder-tree sweetly smells, and where the grass is wetted by the tears of the mourners; and, growing homesick for his garden, Death floated, like a cold, white mist, out of the window.

Or the opening of the great tale, 'The Bell':

In the narrow streets of the big city, in the evening when the sun set and the clouds glistened like gold up among the chimneys, first one person and then another would hear a strange sound, like the pealing of a church bell.

And the end:

And they ran forward to meet each other, and clasped each other by the hand in the great temple of Nature and poetry; and over their heads pealed the invisible holy bell, while blessed spirits danced airily round them to the sound of a jubilant hallelujah.

The surviving manuscripts show how thoroughly Andersen worked at his texts, shaping and polishing them over and over again. In humour and satire he is Dickens's peer, though he paints on a smaller canvas. The ironic asides, the sly allusions and the incidental satire and caricatures have already been referred to. He is a master, likewise, of deadly little thrusts at materialism and philistinism which abound in the fairy tales. 'My fairy tales were for all age-groups, and humour was the salt in them.' Humour, indeed, is continually breaking in even amid the sentiment – with exceptions like 'The Little Mermaid'.

Fairy tales! With its overtones of the nursery, the term is misleading. The Danish word *eventyr* (cognate with the German *Abenteuer* and English 'adventure') is untranslatable. The first English versions, in an attempt to convey the sense of the original title, were called 'wonderful stories'. An *eventyr* may be any sort of fantastic or fabulous tale, not necessarily for children: for example, Shakespeare's *Vintereventyr* (*The Winter's Tale*), Dickens's *Juleeventyr* (*A Christmas Carol*) and *Hoffmanns Eventyr* (*The Tales of Hoffmann,* the opera). 'Tales' would have been appropriate in the case of Andersen's *eventyr*. The original sub-title, 'told for children', incidentally, was soon dropped; and as some of the tales grew to short-story length, Andersen began to call them 'stories' (*historier*). The collected edition of *Eventyr og Historier* comprises 156 titles, and there are a few variants. They are unequal in length and quality. In fact, only about a third of the tales represent Andersen at his

Thumbelina; by Vilhelm Pedersen

The Shadow; by Vilhelm Pedersen

greatest, and most of these date from his middle period, around the 1840's and 1850's. There is some gold, and much dross, dating from later years, and there are some fine tales which date from the early period, the 1830's, among them 'The Emperor's New Clothes', 'The Steadfast Tin Soldier' and 'The Flying Trunk'.

The great decade begins with the publication, for the New Year of 1840, of *Picture Book without Pictures*, a collection of prose poems, 'told by the moon', that are related in style and spirit to the fairy tales and also include small travel sketches. 'The Nightingale', 'Sweethearts' and 'The Ugly Duckling' appeared in 1843. Two of the greatest tales, 'The Snow Queen' and 'The Fir Tree', came in 1844. Another, 'The Bell', a poetic parable about the quest for truth in nature, was published in 1845 along with three of the wittiest, 'The Darning Needle', 'The Jumpers' and 'The Shep⁄herdess and the Chimney Sweep', and a major serious tale, 'The Little Match Girl'. Another masterpiece, 'The Shadow', a black comment on the canonization of the second⁄rate, possibly also a judgment on Andersen's relations with Edvard Collin, appeared in 1847. 'The Old House', 'The Happy Family', 'The Collar' and 'The Story of a Mother' came out in 1848. The best of the later tales include 'It's Perfectly True' and 'The Goblin at the Grocer's', 1852; 'Clodpoll' (a reversion to the early style of 'The Tinder Box' and 'Little Claus and Big Claus'), 1855; 'Father Always Does What's Right' and 'The Snowman', a revealing self⁄portrait, 1861; and 'Hitting on an Idea' and 'The Flea and the Professor', 1872.

The great creative middle period also embraces Andersen's most effective play, *The Mulatto*, and the best travel book, *A Poet's Bazaar*, which have been discussed; the most successful of many

81

William Jerdan

Lady Blessington (standing, right) in female company

other plays, the comedy *The New Confinement Room*, 1849; a short autobiography, *The True Story of My Life*, 1845, written for a German publisher, which was the sketch for his subsequent full-scale autobiography, *The Fairy Tale of My Life*, 1855; and *The Two Baronesses*, 1848, the best novel after *The Improvisatore*. In the same decade he paid the first of his two visits to England.

Anglo-Danish relations were not very intimate in the middle of the nineteenth century, so soon after the Napoleonic Wars, in which Britain and Denmark had fought on opposite sides. There were few literary contacts, and few Danes who knew any English. The chief source and channel of foreign literary influence on Denmark was neighbouring Germany; it was through Germany that Danish literature made its first, and often only, impact abroad. It was into German that Andersen had first been translated, and from German that he had been translated into English. But while still a child, Andersen had, after a fashion, read Shakespeare in translation, and had 'performed' *King Lear* and *The Merchant of Venice* in his puppet theatre. The first novel he had read, at seventeen, had been a translation of Scott's *The Heart of Midlothian*. Walter Scott was to be a major influence on him as a novelist. As we have seen, he had coupled his name with Scott's and Shakespeare's in the pseudonym of his first published work. He had sought to imitate Scott in various other early works. Now, in the space of three years, his first three novels, *A Poet's Bazaar*, the *Picture Book without Pictures* and

a first selection of fairy tales had been published in the land of his two literary idols, and what is more had been highly praised. No other Dane had known such success in England. He therefore needed little persuading by William Jerdan, the editor of *The Literary Gazette*, and his principal promoter in England, to cross the North Sea in order to exploit this initial success and bask in the heart-warming publicity.

Travelling through Germany and Holland, he sailed direct from Rotterdam to London, where he arrived on 23 June 1847, to find himself caught up almost immediately in the social round. On the day following his arrival, the Danish chargé d'affaires got him an invitation to a grand party at Lord Palmerston's, where he received flattering attention from the aristocratic guests, all of whom seemed to have read and have been impressed by *The Improvisatore*. In Lady Blessington's literary salon at Gore House in Kensington, where Jerdan introduced him, he found himself an even greater lion, and there, to his unbounded joy, he met the living English writer whom he admired above any other, Charles Dickens.

The meeting with Dickens, himself a warm admirer of Andersen's work, was unquestionably the highlight of this whole visit for Andersen, and he was 'overjoyed' when Dickens, calling at his hotel in his absence, left an illustrated edition of his works, inscribed in each of the twelve volumes, 'from his friend and admirer Charles Dickens'. Jenny Lind, too, was in London at the time,

Andersen in 1845

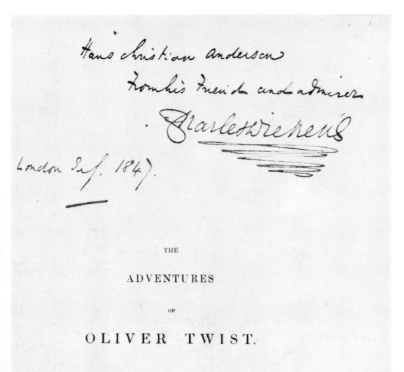

Inscription by Dickens in *Oliver Twist*

appearing with great success in Italian opera at Her Majesty's Theatre, and Andersen saw a good deal of her both on stage and at her furnished house in Old Brompton, where again there was a chaperon present. Again it must have been with mixed feelings that he found his name frequently coupled with hers in the papers.

As several entries in his diary record, Andersen was impressed with the friendliness of everyone he spoke to in shops and in the streets; 'even the police' were courteous. On Ørsted's recommendation, he had put up at the Sablonnière Hotel, a famous French resort of English gourmets, though by this time a little past its prime, perhaps. At any rate, the chargé d'affaires told him to say that he was staying at the legation, as the address was no longer fashionable. Andersen, indeed, soon realized that the area was a haunt of prostitutes; but the hotel was conveniently situated, and he stayed on there. Lady Blessington, aged 58, and living openly with her daughter's husband, the Count d'Orsay, was not 'fashionable' either, he was told; an icy silence would follow whenever he mentioned her name in fashionable company. But he was grateful to her

Richard Bentley

Edinburgh: view from the castle

for having introduced him to Dickens, and spoke up loyally on her behalf.

The July heat and all the socializing, which included visits to his translator, Mary Howitt, at Clapton (a hot journey by omnibus) and his publisher, Richard Bentley, at Sevenoaks (by carriage and train), became rather wearing, and after seven weeks in London Andersen looked forward to his projected visit to Scotland. With Joseph Hambro, a Danish banker who had settled in London, he took train for Edinburgh, where he arrived, after an overnight stop at York, on 11 August. To find himself in the land of Walter Scott, 'land of the mountain and the flood', was like the fulfilment of a dream, and he was soon absorbed in visiting scenes made familiar to him through *The Heart of Midlothian*. With the Hambros he also toured the Highlands, taking in the Rob Roy country, sailing on Loch Katrine, Loch Lomond and the Clyde, and finally leaving for London by train again on 25 August. It had been a tiring two weeks, and to his intense regret he had been too exhausted to make the intended journey to Scott's Abbotsford.

37 albion Street, Broadstairs
(next door but one to the albion Hotel)
Thirtieth august 1847.

My dear andersen.

I am delighted to receive
your cordial note. We are crowded
together here — wife, children, and all — in
a little house on the seashore. Come
and look at us _____ first (look yourself)
to day, and share our family dinner.
We have nobody staying with us but
Mr Stone, a clever artist; and we shall
all be heartily pleased to see you.

When you come back to England
— which you must take an oath to day,
to do soon — I shall hope to see you often

in my own house in London, where I have a
few little pictures and so forth, that I
hope may interest you. But wheresoever
you are, believe that I always am

Your friend and admirer

Charles Dickens

Hans christian andersen.

Letter from Dickens

Leaving London on 29 August by train for Tonbridge, he stayed the night at Bentley's in Sevenoaks, and going on from there by train the next day to Ramsgate, found awaiting him at his hotel a letter from Dickens, inviting him to dinner at Broadstairs. He spent an enjoyable evening with the whole Dickens family. His first visit to England ended magically for him the next day, 31 August, when Dickens, to his delighted surprise, turned up at the quayside, having walked over from Broadstairs to see him off. He stood waving a last goodbye as Andersen's ship sailed out of Ramsgate harbour, bound for Ostend.

In November that year Andersen wrote to Bentley, suggesting that he should publish a small volume of five tales which he had just completed. He wanted to call the little volume *A Christmas Greeting to My English Friends*, and in order to forestall pirated editions, neither author nor publisher being at that time protected by international copyright, he offered to withhold publication in Danish and German until six weeks after the book's appearance in English. Bentley jumped at the offer; and though he did not receive the manuscript until 15 December, succeeded in getting the volume out between Christmas and the New Year. As the copy ran a little short, he included two earlier tales he had meant to publish in his magazine, *Bentley's Miscellany* – 'The Old Street Lamp' and 'The Shadow'.

The five new ones, translated like the others by Charles Beckwith Lohmeyer, an Englishman living in Copenhagen who had translated *A Poet's Bazaar*, were 'The Old House', 'The Drop of Water', 'The Story of a Mother', 'The Collar' and 'The Happy Family'. They were some of Andersen's best tales. The last of them, a delightful fable, like some others of Andersen's best too little known in English, was written at 'the French hotel' in Leicester Square, and has echoes of the London visit. The 'happy family', the snails, live in a forest of butterburs, which had 'been planted for their sakes', in order that they might go to the manor house and be cooked and laid on a silver dish, 'which was supposed to be

Broadstairs in 1865

delicious and extremely fashionable', though what happened after that they did not know. The little volume was dedicated to Dickens, to whom Bentley sent a copy at Andersen's request. Dickens wrote thanking Andersen warmly for the 'dearly prized remembrance' and telling him to 'come over to England again soon'.

Andersen had taken with him to England the first half of a novel that he had worked on for the past four years, but he had been too occupied to write more than a chapter or so during his stay. Ten years had gone by since the publication of his last novel, and many things had conspired to delay completion of this one: successive volumes of fairy tales, now established, with the public and in his own estimation, as his greatest achievement; several minor plays; the short autobiography; a failed poetic drama, *Ahasueras*, about the Wandering Jew, which had possessed him off and on for years; a second visit to Italy in 1845–46; and now the journey to England and Scotland. He finished his new novel, *The Two Baronesses,* in the course of the year following his return from London, and Richard Bentley published it in September 1848, three months before the Danish edition, so as to thwart pirated editions as before.

Andersen's best novel since *The Improvisatore*, *The Two Baronesses* is set partly in Denmark and partly in the Frisian Islands. The second half, which he wrote after his visit to England and Scotland, is clearly inspired by impressions of the Scott country, and by Andersen's favourite novel, *The Heart of Midlothian*. The fine descriptive writing is in the best Scott tradition, and part of the plot is borrowed from Scott and invested with Andersenian auto-biographical features. As before, however, Andersen fails in the larger, epic form, and is seldom good in the development of character. At the same time, he shows himself to be a better realist than Scott. The old baroness, the best-drawn character in the book, epitomizes Andersen's own philosophy; although she has suc-ceeded, through her beauty and intelligence, in marrying into the aristocracy, she can never forget her lowly origins, any more than Andersen could forget his, or the social injustice under which her peasant father had been brutally ill-treated by her father-in-law to be, because he had been unable to pay the rent. Thus, once again, Andersen, peasant by birth, aristocrat by inclination, speaks up for the poor and oppressed. In at least one important respect, he did not share the outlook of his idol and fellow-romantic, Scott: he had no reverence for the past. All his novels were set in his own time. To him, the good old days were bad old days; although far from perfect, the human condition was a great deal better than it used to be, and with the help of the increasing enlightenment and new and developing wonders of science, would become even better in the future.

Gad's Hill Place

Andersen wrote two more novels: *To Be or Not to Be* (1857), and *Lucky Peter* (1870). The former sketches, not very successfully, a young man's religious development from atheistic materialism to an undogmatic form of Christianity, to which Andersen himself inclined in his last years; while the latter is the story of a young singer who dies at the moment of his greatest success, just as Andersen himself might have done. Both novels have the same faults of weak character development and poor plotting; but, like previous novels, both contain many vivid incidents, landscape descriptions and other details that are reminiscent of the fairy tales.

Andersen and Dickens had exchanged letters, and in April 1857 Dickens wrote to say that he had just finished *Little Dorrit,* and, now that he was 'a free man', invited Andersen to come and stay with him at his new house, that is to say Gad's Hill Place, in June. Few things could have given greater pleasure than the cordially phrased invitation from Andersen's most admired contemporary, whose friendship he cherished as the outstanding event of his first visit to England ten years before. It was therefore in the happiest of moods that he left Denmark at the beginning of June

89

and, travelling through Holland and France, crossed from Calais to Dover on 11 June. Changing trains at London Bridge, he 'sped past towns and villages, the train hugging the Thames which, crowded with sails and steamers, glistened on our left', as far as Higham in Kent. There a porter, who had been told to look out for him, took charge of his luggage, and together they walked between hedges of honeysuckle and wild roses the two miles to Gad's Hill, to be received by Dickens and his family.

It was a glorious summer that year in the 'Garden of England' and Andersen made many expeditions of discovery in the surrounding countryside with the Dickenses, who had moved into their new home just a fortnight before. Sometimes he would go up to London either with Dickens or by himself, in the latter case occasionally getting lost, or would accompany Dickens as far as Rochester, which he would then explore on his own. One afternoon Dickens took him to the Crystal Palace on its new site in Sydenham Park, where they heard a choir of 2,500 voices sing *The Messiah,* and then on to the Lyceum Theatre to see a visiting Italian star, Ristori. Not surprisingly after this heavy feast, Andersen was too exhausted to make his almost invariable diary entry that night.

On another occasion, he saw Dickens perform, with Wilkie Collins and Mark Lemon, the editor of *Punch,* in a benefit production of Collins's *The Frozen Deep,* in aid of the widow of Douglas Jerrold, the playwright, a performance that was attended by Queen Victoria, Prince Albert, the King of the Belgians and a glittering array of other royal personages. 'Dickens acted with moving sincerity and great dramatic genius', Andersen wrote. 'He was a quite remarkable actor, so free from the mannerisms that one sees in tragic parts in England and France.' After the show, Andersen joined the company in a champagne supper at the offices of Dickens's magazine, *Household Words*. In London, he also attended the first performances of Charles Kean's spectacular production of *The Tempest* at the Princess's Theatre, and thought that the play had been swamped in the lavish setting. 'A work by Shakespeare, when artistically presented only between three flats, I find more enjoyable than here, where it was lost in the beautiful decor.'

Much as he enjoyed the richness and variety of London, Andersen was always glad to get 'home', as he said, to Gad's Hill and the Dickens family circle. Home life, next to appreciation, was what he always longed for most, and envied intensely in those who had it. The friendship and esteem shown by Dickens on the previous visit had been heart-warming; admission to his fireside now was bliss, and he revelled in it. The affection was reciprocated up to a point, but could never go as deep on Dickens's side. There can be no

Wilkie Collins

(*Below*) Dickens photographed with his family and friends during rehearsals of *The Frozen Deep*

doubt that Dickens genuinely admired Andersen the writer, and the Dickens family could not help being fascinated by this strange foreign visitor, with his funny incomprehensible English, the charming little posies which he gathered for them in the woods, and the intricate and beautiful paper cuts that he was so skilled in making. But there were difficulties. Dickens's son, Sir Henry Dickens, has left a description of both the pleasures and the irritations of Andersen's stay in their midst:

He turned out to be a lovable and yet a somewhat uncommon and strange personality. His manner was delightfully simple, such as one rather expected from the delicacy of his work. He was necessarily very interesting, but he was certainly somewhat of an 'oddity'. In person, tall, gaunt, rather ungainly; in manner, thoughtful and agreeable. He had one beautiful accomplishment, which was the cutting out in paper, with an ordinary pair of scissors, of little figures of sprites and elves, gnomes, fairies and animals of all kinds which might well have stepped out of the pages of his books.... Much as there was in him to like and admire, he was, on the other hand, most decidedly disconcerting in his general manner, for he used constantly to be doing things, quite unconsciously, which might almost be called 'gauche': so much so that I am afraid the small boys in the family rather laughed at him behind his back; but, so far as the members of the family were concerned, he was treated with the utmost consideration and courtesy.

(*Below and opposite*) Two of Andersen's paper-cuts

Dickens, too, while he always treated Andersen with the same consideration and courtesy, could not resist poking fun at him in letters to friends. 'We are suffering a good deal from Andersen', he wrote to Angela Burdett-Coutts. 'The other day we lost him when he came up to London Bridge Terminus, and he took a cab by himself. The cabman driving him through the new unfinished street at Clerkenwell, he thought was driving him into remote fastnesses, to rob and murder him. He consequently arrived here with all his money, his watch, his pocket book, and documents, *in his boots* – and it was a tremendous business to unpack him and get them off.' And when Andersen departed, Dickens put up a card over the dressing-table mirror: 'Hans Andersen slept in this room for five weeks – which seemed to the family AGES!'

Andersen's oddities and unpredictable moods – as when Mrs Dickens found him prostrated on the lawn after reading a bad review of *To Be or Not To Be* – together with his characteristic hypochondria and often unintelligible English, made him, of course, a difficult guest to have about the house, and he grossly outstayed his welcome. He had come for a fortnight, and lingered on for five weeks, feeling at home, and probably interpreting conventional politeness for pressing invitations to remain. Moreover, the visit had come at a difficult time for Dickens: there were financial pressures, and all the business connected with the unexpected death of Douglas Jerrold and the benefit performance. Worse, a crisis was brewing in the family, and only weeks after Andersen's visit the marriage broke up. Of this he was blissfully unaware: 'the family life seems so harmonious', he wrote to a friend. Dickens and his wife remained friendly and considerate to the end. When he eventually left, Dickens personally drove him in his trap to Maidstone for the Folkestone train, drew a map of the route showing the stations, and embraced him warmly on departure. They were never to meet again.

Dickens wrote a friendly, if perhaps superficially conventional, letter in reply to two effusive letters of thanks from Andersen; but he did not reply to Andersen's later letters, and, realizing that the friendship had come to an end, Andersen stopped writing himself. 'All, all over, and that's the way of every story', he wrote in his autobiography, quoting the ending of his fairy tale 'The Fir Tree'. The friendship had meant a good deal more to Andersen, the lonely bachelor thirsting for companionship, than it had meant to the convivial family man Dickens. It had also provided evidence, for those in Denmark who were still unconvinced, of Andersen's reputation abroad. It remained a sad but treasured memory; always in after-years, Andersen spoke in admiration and affection of Dickens, never bitterly.

'Homage to Hans Christian Andersen'; cartoon from *Punch*, 1857

The two visits to England were part of a continuing and seemingly triumphal progress through Europe at this time and later. From the mid-1830's, Andersen had stayed with increasing frequency as a guest at various country mansions, thirty or so in all. There, in those days of home entertainment, he would read his latest tales to the family, while finding temporary peace and repose for further writing in pleasant surroundings, indulged in by his hostess and waited on by liveried servants. The royal family itself bestowed various personal favours on him. On several occasions he stayed as the guest of the Duke and Duchess of Augustenburg in Schleswig. In 1844, Christian VIII, who as Crown Prince Christian Frederik had received him in audience at Odense Castle more than twenty-five years before, invited him to stay with the queen and himself at their country residence on one of the Frisian Islands, in Holstein. He spent some ten days with them, dining regularly with

Andersen photographed at Frijsenborg
Manor in 1865

the royal party, and reading his fairy tales to them after dinner. The
visit provided background material for *The Two Baronesses*. The
friendly relations were kept up. 'Where are you dining tonight?
Nowhere in particular? Then, why not come round to the palace
and have dinner with my wife and me?' Relations with Christian's
successor, Frederik VII, were just as warm.

Further afield, Andersen found particular favour in the royal
courts of Germany, which became regular stopping-places on his
itineraries. In 1846 he received the first of many decorations, German and Danish, when Wilhelm IV of Prussia invited him to dine

Andersen reading to the Duke of Augustenburg and his family in 1845

at Potsdam and awarded him the Order of the Red Eagle: on Jonas Collin's birthday, Andersen gratefully recorded. That same year he spent a month at Weimar, where he had formed a lifelong friendship with the hereditary duke, later ruling grand duke, Carl Alexander of Saxe-Weimar-Eisenach. The court at Weimar had gained renown through its patronage of Goethe and Schiller, and some of the lustre dating from that time still surrounded it. On his way home from England in 1857, Andersen paid one of many later visits to Weimar in order to attend the unveiling of Goethe's and Schiller's statues. Carl Alexander kept up a cordial correspondence with Andersen over many years. Overhearing at his court a sarcastic remark about Andersen's vanity, after Andersen's death, he observed sharply: 'Hans Christian Andersen was a great writer, a delightful man and my good friend.'

Wherever Andersen went on these tireless travels, he never failed to seek out the leading literary and artistic personalities: Tieck, Chamisso, Heine, Eckermann, Humboldt, the Grimms, Schumann, Mendelssohn, Spohr, Liszt, Victor Hugo, Dumas *père*, Lamartine, de Vigny and the actress Rachel are among the many whom he met at one time or another. The final two-thirds of the autobiography *The Fairy Tale of My Life* is a long and repetitious chronicle of such meetings, honours, distinctions, achievements and successes. The truth is not so simple. For a necessary corrective, one must turn to the confessional diaries and Andersen's voluminous

Opposite:

(*Above left*) Weimar in 1846

(*Above right*) Carl Alexander, Grand Duke of Saxe-Weimar-Eisenach (1818–1901)

(*Below*) Score autographed by Schumann for Andersen

correspondence, and to those 'unofficial' autobiographies, the fairy tales themselves.

As we have seen, Andersen never stopped telling his own story; that was the way he abreacted. Sometimes he tells it in an idealized form, sometimes with self-revelatory candour. In tale after tale – 'The Tinder Box', 'Little Claus and Big Claus', 'The Steadfast Tin Soldier', 'The Swineherd', 'The Ugly Duckling' – he is the hero, who triumphs over poverty, persecution and plain stupidity, and who sometimes, in reversal of the facts, marries the princess ('Clodpoll') or scorns her ('The Swineherd'). In 'Little Ida's Flowers' he is the jolly student ,'who could tell the loveliest of stories and cut out such amusing pictures: of hearts with little dancing ladies in them, flowers, and big palaces with doors you could open'. In 'The Naughty Boy', written after his rejection by Louise Collin, he is the old poet who is shot through the heart by Cupid as he sits by his fireside. Louise is the prince in 'The Little Mermaid', as Andersen himself is the mermaid. Riborg Voigt appears with Andersen in 'Sweethearts'; Andersen and Jenny Lind in 'The Nightingale'; and Andersen and Kierkegaard in 'The Snail and the Rosebush'. 'The Shadow' probably alludes, in part, to the relations of Andersen and Edvard Collin, with Andersen as the poet and Collin as the shadow.

Andersen reading to the children of a friend

Andersen: a photograph taken at
Munich in 1860

Other tales are replies to critics; such as the bitter 'Hitting on an
Idea', the story of a young academic who studies in order to be⁄
come a poet by Easter, and get married and live on his poetry, but
who fails to hit on an idea even by Whitsun and so becomes a critic
and hits out at poets at Shrovetide instead ('one of the experienced
tales', Andersen wrily remarks, in his notes to the collected edition).
The satirical tale of the matches, inserted in 'The Flying Trunk',
is about the Heiberg literary circle, and was meant to be read by
Mrs Heiberg in her salon, at a party which had to be called off.
The Heiberg literary conventions are also, in part, the butt in 'The
Nightingale'. In 'The Galoshes of Fortune', Heiberg is satirized
as a parrot. At least as true to the facts of Andersen's life as 'The Ugly
Duckling', and more profound, is 'The Fir Tree', one of the out⁄
standing tales, dating from Andersen's maturest period in the
1840's.

Andersen's study

This brilliant piece throws light on the doubts and insecurity which often lay behind the glitter and the glory that are paraded in *The Fairy Tale of My Life*. The fir-tree grew up in the woods, in warm sunshine and fresh air, but hated to be called a 'pretty little tree' and wanted to grow into a big tree like all the others. When it saw them being chopped down, it envied them their interesting new experience, and could hardly wait for next Christmas to come round, when it in its turn would 'go on a journey'. In the event, to stand in a room carrying hot candles which burnt down to its branches was an unpleasant experience, and it longed to be back in the open air again. Always yearning for something fresh, never happy in the present, looking back on the events of yesterday with melancholy nostalgia, it went finally to its fate, which was to be chopped up and burnt in the copper, while the smallest of the boys playing in the yard wore on his breast the gold star which the tree had borne on Christmas Eve, 'the happiest evening of its life', though this it had never realized at the time. 'Now that was all over, and it was all over with the tree, and the story's over as well! All, all over! And that's the way of every story!'

The story of the fir-tree, suffering incessantly from 'bark-ache', is palpably a self-portrait, drawn with merciless candour. Its history is Andersen's. When everything seemed to be going his way, when at long last he had won recognition and fame, and honours and distinctions were being bestowed upon him from all sides, there remained always this constant ache, an acute sense of deprivation. Looking before and after, pining for what was not, he perpetually chased a happiness which seemed always, except at fleeting but glorious moments, to elude him. When not on one of his long journeys abroad, he spent the winter in his furnished rooms in Copenhagen, moving at intervals and staying in between at hotels.

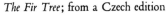

The Fir Tree; from a Czech edition

He would lunch alone, and dine regularly on fixed evenings at the homes of friends – the Collins on Mondays, Ørsted's on Tuesdays, and so on. The evenings after dinner he would spend at the theatre – my club' – where he had his allotted seat. With the return of spring he would pack his bags and be off, going to one of the manor houses or perhaps to Germany, stopping on the way to visit friends in the provinces, but never staying anywhere long. 'Alas, why can I never enjoy the present?' he asked a friend.

It has been suggested, on superficial grounds, that Andersen was homosexual. He never married; there were feminine traits in his character; he behaved, and expressed himself in letters, emotionally, even ecstatically. Neither severally nor collectively are these characteristics proof of sexual inversion. The superlative expressions of affection were applied fairly indiscriminately. To some extent, they reflect a sense of social and emotional inferiority, obviously so in relation to the well-bred, emotionally controlled and self-assured Edvard Collin, for example. They also indicate a deep and genuine

Glorup Manor, where Andersen wrote some of his tales

Andersen and Jonas Collin, the younger, in 1863

(*Opposite*) Andersen photographed by Theodor Collin

sense of gratitude, mixed probably with some snobbishness, for the patronage and friendship of the exalted rich, as in the case of the grand duke of Saxe-Weimar-Eisenach. The Collins knew Andersen intimately. He had grown up in the family and had been under their daily observation for many years. Perfectly normal, as well as eminently respectable, themselves, they were also intelligent and perceptive. Had there been the merest shadow of suspicion of homosexuality in Andersen, they would never have allowed their young sons to accompany him on long journeys abroad, as several of them did; Edvard's son, Jonas 'the younger', went with him on three occasions, to Italy, Spain and elsewhere.

Edvard Collin's house in Copenhagen

(*Below*) Edvard Collin and his family

Andersen in the gardens of
Frijsenborg Manor in 1868

At the same time, there is plenty of evidence of Andersen's attraction to women. The reality of his feelings for Riborg Voigt seems beyond dispute, even though, for complex reasons, he failed to press his claims with her. Nor were they any less real, if less intense, in the other cases: Louise Collin, Jenny Lind and the rest. Likewise, there is plenty of evidence that women could be attracted by Andersen, in spite of his *gaucheries*, though never enough for any of them to want to marry him; they all preferred more normal, more ordinary and psychologically less demanding men. Doubtless he understood; but he grieved none the less.

The temptation to find satisfaction in casual relations, as a few of his gayer companions tried to persuade him to do, could be urgent in the warm south; in Rome and Naples, for instance. The relevant entries in his diaries imply heterosexual relations. But the psychological inhibitions were stronger. Moral and ethical scruples, no doubt, were uppermost among these. Andersen's extreme fastidiousness, his acute awareness of dirt and disease, must have been another strong deterrent, as suggested by this entry in his diary, under Rome, 3 June 1841: 'Jerichau called: he told me of his ailments and complaints. One of them shall be in my thoughts when sin shows to me its fruit of knowledge.' No less compelling was the sexual timidity, the emotional immaturity one may say, which made him recoil in the case of Riborg Voigt. At any rate he abstained: Andersen remained a bachelor and, we can be sure, celibate till the end of his days. His 'sin' was masturbation; he wrestled vainly and wretchedly with it, and suffered agonies of remorse and self-reproach.

Andersen was a sick man, of course, and he knew it. 'Bear with me,' he wrote to a friend, 'you know I have a screw loose.' 'Oh, if only some doctor could tell me what is wrong with me!' he exclaimed on another occasion. There was none at that time; and all that his friends and family doctor, Theodor Collin, could do in the circumstances was to console and encourage him and help him to get over his blacker moods, which became more frequent in his old age. If they often succeeded, and bore with him as he asked, it was because there was a balancing side of his personality, the determination that had always seen him through in the end, together with the wit and humour which both appealed to and enchanted his friends and enabled him to laugh and poke fun at himself. They were the characteristics that saved him, in spite of everything, from the fate, so greatly feared, of his grandfather; these and their successful transference to his writings. He survived because he knew supremely well how to abreact. 'Forgive me for having talked so much of my "case", but ... if I may not talk about my pains, I have no pleasure in them.' His letters abound in such flashes of self-knowledge; written after the initial, despairing reactions that are recorded in the

(*Opposite*) A reading of the fairy tales at Frijsenborg Manor in 1863

The torchlight procession on the occasion of Andersen's appointment as honorary citizen of Odense

(*Opposite*) The diploma making Andersen an honorary citizen of Odense

diaries, they indicate the reassertion of his healthy good humour and high spirits. Occasionally, the healing self-irony even comes out in the diaries, as in the entry: 'I am tired of life – tonight!' More than anywhere, he abreacted in his works, and so, in his characteristic phrase, 'got his money back'. 'How have you worked yourself into such a good humour? you ask. I am sustained by a natural mental health, and have written myself into good heart.'

The climax of Andersen's fascinating career came on 6 December 1867, when the city council of Odense, from where he had set out to 'become famous', on his first journey long ago, made him an honorary citizen, amid great celebration. The day was declared a school holiday, and the proceedings included a banquet, much speech-making and a torchlight procession. The crowning triumph of the occasion was that the whole city was illuminated in his honour, exactly as the old woman had foretold more than half a century before; though the fulfilment was a little less miraculous than might appear, since there had been some nudging of fate, the prophecy having been well publicized in *The Fairy Tale of My Life* and on other occasions. As always, Andersen's joy in the achievement was marred, this time, in a way that was typically tragi-comic, by a raging toothache, brought on by nerves. Typically again,

(*Above*) A late photograph of
Andersen in his Copenhagen home

Mrs Dorothea Melchior

At Rolighed

Moritz Melchior

however, he 'got his money back', in the ruefully comic tale of 'Aunty Toothache', one of the last that he wrote.

Andersen grew old before his time. His black moods became more frequent and prolonged, being often accompanied by nightmares, in which he would be plagued by Meisling and other early tormenters. Old Jonas Collin and his wife had long been dead, and most of their children, Andersen's contemporaries, were married and had families of their own. The old 'home of homes' had ceased to exist. But Edvard still managed Andersen's business affairs, and through shrewd investment had secured him a comfortable fortune. He still dined once a week, on regular evenings, at Edvard's, with Louise and her family and with Ørsted's widow. But now there were other friends, and another 'home of homes'.

The intimate friends of Andersen's last years, and a great support to him in his old age, were Moritz Melchior, a banker and wealthy merchant, and, especially, his wife Dorothea. They came together

113

for musical evenings at first, and soon he was dining regularly at their flat in town. He spent part of the summer at their villa Rolighed – 'Quietude' – just outside the city, and in time they gave him his own rooms, with a balcony which overlooked the beautiful Sound, and a servant to attend to him day and night. In Andersen's declining years, Dorothea Melchior proved herself both a loyal friend and comforter, and finally a tireless nurse. In his blackest moods he would send for young Jonas Collin, with whom he planned, almost to the end, to make another journey abroad. But his earthly journeys were over. He died at Rolighed, on 4 August 1875, of cancer of the liver, four months after his seventieth birthday.

Statue in a Copenhagen park

CHRONOLOGY

1805 2 April. Hans Christian Andersen born at Odense, Denmark, the only son of Hans Andersen, shoemaker, and his wife, Anne Marie Andersdatter.

1819 September. Goes to Copenhagen to 'seek his fortune' on the stage. Finds well-wishers who support him and give him lessons.

1821 Obtains small part at theatre, is admitted to song school and has first crude play rejected.

1822 October. Is given place at Slagelse state grammar school.

1828 First poem published. Passes university entrance examination.

1829 Publishes *A Walking Tour* and has first play, *Love on St Nicholas Church Tower*, produced.

1830 First volume of poems published. Visits Jutland. Falls in love with Riborg Voigt.

1831 Travels in Germany and publishes *Shadow Pictures of a Journey to the Harz Mountains and Saxony*.

1833 Publishes *Collected Poems*. Travels via Germany and Paris to Italy, spending six months in Rome.

1835 Publishes his first novel, *The Improvisatore*, and the first fairy tales.

1836 Second novel, *O.T.*, published.

1837 Third novel, *Only a Fiddler*, published. Fairy tales begin to appear in annual volumes.

1840 *Picture Book without Pictures* published and most successful play, *The Mulatto*, produced.

1841–2 Travels in the Balkans. *A Poet's Bazaar* published in 1842.

1843 Falls in love with Jenny Lind.

1845 Consolidates friendship with Grand Duke Carl Alexander at Weimar and is decorated by the king of Prussia at Potsdam. *The Improvisatore, O.T., Only a Fiddler* and a first volume of fairy tales published in England.

1847 Visits England and Scotland and meets Charles Dickens.

1848 Publishes his fourth novel, *The Two Baronesses*.

1851 Publishes the travel book *In Sweden*.

1855 *The Fairy Tale of My Life* published.

1857 Visits London and stays with Dickens at Gad's Hill. Publishes novel *To Be or Not To Be*.

1861 Pays another visit to Rome.

1862 Visits Spain and Tangier. First collected edition of *Fairy Tales and Stories* published.

1863 Publishes *In Spain*.

1866 Travels in Portugal.

1867 Made an honorary citizen of Odense.

1868 Publishes *In Portugal, 1866*.

1870 Last novel, *Lucky Peter*, published.

1872 Last fairy tales published.

1874 Second collected edition of *Fairy Tales and Stories* published.

1875 4 August. Dies near Copenhagen.

NOTES ON THE PICTURES

Frontispiece: HANS CHRISTIAN ANDERSEN. *Photo: Danish Tourist Board*

5 VIEW OF ODENSE, 1805. Coloured engraving by S.L. Lange. Royal Library, Copenhagen

6 THE FLAKHAVEN SQUARE in Odense, in the year 1811. In the background is St Knud's Church, where Andersen was confirmed. Watercolour by H.C. Roulund. Odense City Museums

7 ILLUSTRATION from Andersen's tale *She was Good for Nothing* by Vilhelm Pedersen. Odense City Museums. *Photo Royal Danish Ministry of Foreign Affairs*

8 VIEW of the square, Klingenberg, Odense. Oil painting dating from the 1840's. Andersen lived in this part of Odense as a child, in Munkemøllestræde, which joins Klingenberg to the right. In the centre is the grammar school and St Knud's Church. Odense City Museums

9 ANDERSEN's traditional birthplace, Odense. Lithograph, 1868. Odense City Museums

10 VIEW of the street, Klaregade, Odense. On the left is Odense gaol, mentioned in *The Fairy Tale of my Life*, which gave the title to the novel *O.T.* In the background is the river and on the right the bishop's palace. Oil painting by shoemaker J.P. Thomsen (b. 1815), when young. Odense City Museums

IN THE COBBLER Hans Andersen's house, Odense. *Photo the author*

11 ANDERSEN HOUSE in Munkemøllestræde, Odense. Watercolour by J.T. Hanck, 1836. Odense City Museums

MUNKEMØLLE, near Odense. Watercolour by J.T. Hanck, 1831. Odense City Museums

12 SPANISH and French troops in Denmark. Drawing by A. Ørnstrup, 1808. Royal Library, Copenhagen

13 BOMBARDMENT of Copenhagen, 3–4 September 1807. Painting by C.V. Eckersberg. Frederiksborg Museum, Copenhagen

14 VIEW of the canal, Odense. Engraving by J. T. Hanck after H. A. Grosch. Royal Library, Copenhagen

15 ODENSE THEATRE. Lithograph printed by J. Hesse, Berlin. *Photo Royal Danish Ministry of Foreign Affairs*

ODENSE charity school. Odense City Museums

16 THE GOOSEBERRY BUSH and modern commemorative tablet, Andersen house in Munkemøllestræde. *Photo the author*

17 NAPOLEON I on horseback. Coloured print from Andersen's childhood. Odense City Museums

KNUD HJALLESE, a grenadier of the King's Own regiment. Coloured pen drawing, early nineteenth century. Andersen's father joined the same regiment as a musketeer, 1812–14. Odense City Museums

18 BY THE RIVER, Odense, 11 June 1816. Drawing by J. T. Hanck. National Museum, Copenhagen

19 WASHING PLACE, Odense, where Andersen's mother used to do her washing. Odense City Museums. *Photo Royal Danish Ministry of Foreign Affairs*

20 POEM by Andersen *In Memory of Little Maria's Death, 26 November 1816.* Pasted into Andersen's album, and composed by him at the age of twelve, 17 March 1817. *Photo Royal Danish Ministry of Foreign Affairs*

22 VIEW of Overgade, the old centre of Odense, seen from Korsgade. Coloured pen drawing, *c.* 1840. Odense City Museums

ANDERSEN'S DEPARTURE from Odense. Modern fresco by Larsen Stevns. Odense City Museums

23 ANNA MARGRETHE SCHALL (1775–1852), whom Andersen met on 7 September 1819. *Photo Royal Danish Ministry of Foreign Affairs*

24 AT THE THEATRE, Copenhagen. Contemporary engraving. Statens Museum for Kunst, Copenhagen.

25 GIUSEPPE SIBONI (1780–1839). Painting by D. Monies. Frederiksborg Museum, Copenhagen

26 THE COMPOSER Professor C. E. F. Weyse (1774–1842). Odense City Museums

27 THE STREET in Copenhagen where Andersen lived during his first stay there. Coloured drawing by L. Both, 1884. Royal Library, Copenhagen

28 SLAGELSE in 1824. Royal Library, Copenhagen

29 JONAS COLLIN (1776–1861). Odense City Museums. *Photo Royal Danish Ministry of Foreign Affairs*

30 SIMON MEISLING. Oil painting. Odense City Museums. *Photo Royal Danish Ministry of Foreign Affairs*

THE GRAMMAR SCHOOL at Slagelse. Odense City Museums

31 ANDERSEN'S examination certificate, 1828. Odense City Museums

32 ST NICHOLAS CHURCH, Copenhagen. Lithograph. Royal Library, Copenhagen

34 RIBORG VOIGT. Odense City Museums. *Photo Royal Danish Ministry of Foreign Affairs*

35 HANS ANDERSEN. Drawing by C. Hartmann. Frederiksborg Museum, Copenhagen

36 POUCH found round Andersen's neck at death, and the note about it by Jonas Collin. Odense City Museums

Bottled up. Drawing by Andersen. This drawing may represent Andersen's hopeless love for Riborg Voigt. Odense City Museums

Gravestone. Drawing by Andersen. Odense City Museums

37 RIBORG VOIGT and her three children. Fåborg Town Museum

FLOWERS given by Andersen to Riborg Voigt and kept by her. Odense City Museums

38 ADELBERT VON CHAMISSO. Engraving after the painting by R. Reinick. Odense City Museums

LUDWIG TIECK. Royal Library, Copenhagen

39 DETAIL of a page from Andersen's diary of his first journey abroad. Royal Library, Copenhagen

Kløversparrude, from the fairy opera *The Raven* by J. P. E. Hartmann and Andersen, 1832, Library of the Royal Theatre, Copenhagen

41 THE COURTYARD of the Collins' house, Bredgade 4, Copenhagen. Engraving after a drawing by H. Hansen, 1850. Royal Library, Copenhagen

SELF-CARICATURE. Odense City Museums

42 HENRIETTE COLLIN (1772–1845), wife of Jonas Collin. Pastel by C. Hornemann. Odense City Museums

THE EXTERIOR of the Collins' house, Bredgade 4. Engraving by H. Hansen, 1853. *Photo Royal Danish Ministry of Foreign Affairs*

43 EDVARD COLLIN (1808–86) and his wife Henriette (1813–94). Odense City Museums. *Photo Royal Danish Ministry of Foreign Affairs*

44 *The Swineherd.* Drawing by V. Pedersen. Odense City Museums

45 LOUISE COLLIN (1813–98). Odense City Museums

46 THE TIBER, Rome. Drawing by Andersen. Odense City Museums

47 TEMPLE at Paestum. Drawing by Andersen. Odense City Museums

AMALFI. Drawing by Andersen. Odense City Museums

THE PONTE VECCHIO, Florence, 12 April 1834. Drawing by Andersen. Odense City Museums

48 Bertel Thorvaldsen (1768–1844). Painting by C. W. Eckersberg. Oil on canvas, 1814. Thorvaldsens Museum, Copenhagen

ANDERSEN IN ROME. Painting by Albert Küchler. Frederiksborg Museum, Copenhagen

THE CAFÉ GRECO in Rome, 1842. Watercolour by L. Passini. Kunsthalle, Hamburg

49 THE SPANISH STEPS, Rome. Drawing by Andersen. *Photo Royal Danish Ministry of Foreign Affairs*

THORVALDSEN'S HOUSE, Via Sistina, Rome. Drawing by Andersen. Odense City Museums

51 VIEW OF NYHAVN, Copenhagen. Drawing by Andersen from his window. Odense City Museums

VIEW OF NYHAVN. Andersen lived at No. 20, one of the houses on the far side of the canal, from 1834 to 1838. From 1872 to 1875 he lived at No. 18 (the higher house on the right). Odense City Museums

52 ANDERSEN. Painting by C. A. Jensen, 1836. This painting was exhibited at the Kunstforening, October 1836. *Photo Royal Danish Ministry of Foreign Affairs*

53 *Little Claus and Big Claus.* Drawing by V. Pedersen for Andersen's fairy tale. Odense City Museums

54 HANS CHRISTIAN ØRSTED (1777–1851). Frederiksborg Museum, Copenhagen

55 TITLE-PAGE of Mathilde Ørsted's copy of a volume of Andersen's tales. *Photo Royal Danish Ministry of Foreign Affairs*

56 SØREN KIERKEGAARD. Drawing done in lamp-black on a slab of pipe-clay, *c.* 1840, by his cousin, N. C. Kierkegaard. Copenhagen City Museum

57 ANDERSEN'S INSCRIPTION to Kierkegaard in a copy of *New Fairy Tales.* Courtesy E. Borup Jensen

59 VIEW OF VESUVIUS. Drawing by Andersen. Odense City Museums

60 CARLSPLATZ in Munich. Drawing by Andersen, Odense City Museums

PORTRAIT of Andersen. Drawing by Adam Muller, *c.* 1833. Odense City Museums

61 ANDERSEN'S Turkish passport. H. C. Andersen's house, Odense. *Photo Royal Danish Ministry of Foreign Affairs*

CAMEL on the Acropolis. Drawing by Andersen. Odense City Museums

WHIRLING DERVISHES at Pera, Constantinople. Drawing by Andersen, Odense City Museums

62 SOME OF ANDERSEN'S belongings in the Odense City Museums, including a coil of rope and trunks. *Photo Royal Danish Ministry of Foreign Affairs*

63 CARICATURE of Andersen and a chestnut-seller in Spain. From *Schwärmer,* 1863. Royal Library, Copenhagen

64 *The Emperor's New Clothes.* Drawing by V. Pedersen for Andersen's fairy story. Odense City Museums. *Photo Royal Danish Ministry of Foreign Affairs*

65 *The Little Mermaid.* Drawing by V. Pedersen for Andersen's fairy tale. Odense City Museums. *Photo Royal Danish Ministry of Foreign Affairs*

67 TITLE-PAGE of the first German edition of the fairy tales, 1839, with drawings by G. Osterwald. Royal Library, Copenhagen

68, 69 DANISH STRIP CARTOON of *The Princess on the Pea.* Odense City Museums. German strip cartoon of *The Steadfast Tin Soldier.* Odense City Museums

70 *The Princess on the Pea.* Page 40 from a Greek edition. British Museum, Department of Printed Books. *Photo R.B. Fleming*

Thumbelina. From a German edition of Andersen's tales. Illustrations by Ludwig Richter and Oscar Pletsch, 1875. British Museum, Department of Printed Books. *Photo R.B. Fleming*

71 CARDBOARD COVER of a French edition of Andersen's tales, published in Tours, 1853. Royal Library, Copenhagen

72 *The Story of a Mother.* Bengali version of Andersen's tale. Royal Library, Copenhagen

73 *The Nightingale.* Drawing by V. Pedersen for Andersen's fairy tale. Royal Library, Copenhagen

75 JENNY LIND, 'the Swedish Nightingale'. *Photo Royal Danish Ministry of Foreign Affairs*

76 THE PANTOMIME THEATRE in the Tivoli Gardens, Copenhagen. Courtesy the Tivoli Gardens

77 *The Ugly Duckling.* Drawing by V. Pedersen for Andersen's fairy tale. Odense City Museums. *Photo Royal Danish Ministry of Foreign Affairs*

78 CHARLES DICKENS. Photograph in Andersen's possession. Odense City Museums

80 *Thumbelina.* Drawing by V. Pedersen. Odense City Museums

81 *The Shadow.* Drawing by V. Pedersen. Odense City Museums

82 WILLIAM JERDAN. From an etching by D. Maclise. *Photo Radio Times Hulton Picture Library*

LADY BLESSINGTON with her literary circle. *Photo Radio Times Hulton Picture Library*

83 *Oliver Twist*, inscribed by Dickens to Andersen, 1847. Royal Library, Copenhagen

ANDERSEN IN 1845. Watercolour by Karl Hartmann. Odense City Museums

84 RICHARD BENTLEY. *Photo Radio Times Hulton Picture Library*

85 VIEW OF EDINBURGH from the castle. Printed by Day and Son from a lithograph by T. Picken after David Roberts. *Photo Radio Times Hulton Picture Library*

86 LETTER FROM DICKENS to Andersen, August 1847. Odense City Museums

87 BROADSTAIRS, 1865. *Photo Radio Times Hulton Picture Library*

89 GAD'S HILL PLACE, Kent. *Photo Radio Times Hulton Picture Library*

91 WILKIE COLLINS. *Photo Radio Times Hulton Picture Library*

GROUP taken in Albert Smith's garden at Walham Green, 1857, during a rehearsal of Collins's *The Frozen Deep. Photo Radio Times Hulton Picture Library*

92 PAPER CUT-OUT by Andersen showing two ballet-dancers on a tight-rope. *Photo Royal Danish Ministry of Foreign Affairs*

93 PAPER CUT-OUT by Andersen showing a dancer and a stork. *Photo Royal Danish Ministry of Foreign Affairs*

94 *Homage to Hans Christian Andersen:* Punch cartoon of 10 January 1857. Odense City Museums

95 PART OF A LETTER from Dickens to William Jerdan describing Andersen's peculiar behaviour during his second visit to Dickens, 1857. From the Suzannet Collection, by permission of the Trustees of the Dickens House. *Photo Eileen Tweedy*

96 ANDERSEN in front of Frijsenborg Manor, 1865. Odense City Museums

97 THE ROYAL PALACE at Copenhagen. Watercolour by H.G.F. Holm, *c.* 1850. Statens Museum for Kunst, Copenhagen

KING CHRISTIAN VIII (1786–1848). Painting by C.A. Jensen. Frederiksborg Museum, Copenhagen

KING FREDERIK VII (1808–63). Painting by F.L. Storch, 1854. Frederiksborg Museum, Copenhagen

98 ANDERSEN READING ALOUD to the Augustenburg family circle, 1845. Frederiksborg Museum, Copenhagen

99 WEIMAR in 1846. Royal Library, Copenhagen

CARL ALEXANDER, Grand Duke of Saxe-Weimar-Eisenach (1818–1901). Odense City Museums

ROBERT SCHUMANN'S autograph for Andersen. Royal Library, Copenhagen

100 ANDERSEN READING ALOUD to the children of Madame Baumann. Painting by Jerichau-Baumannsborn. Odense City Museums

101 ANDERSEN, 1860. H.C. Andersen's house, Odense

102 ANDERSEN'S STUDY. Odense City Museums

103 GLORUP MANOR. The garden front. Lithograph by S.J. Grunvald. Odense City Museums

CZECH VERSION of *The Fir Tree,* printed in Prague, 1874. British Museum, Department of Printed Books. *Photo R.B. Fleming*

104 ANDERSEN and Jonas Collin the younger, 1863. Odense City Museums

105 ANDERSEN photographed by Theodor Collin outside the Collin home. Library of Congress, Washington, D.C.

106 EDVARD COLLIN'S HOUSE, photographed 1880. Royal Library, Copenhagen

EDVARD COLLIN with his family. Royal Library, Copenhagen

107 ANDERSEN IN THE GARDENS of Frijsenborg Manor, 1868. Library of Congress, Washington, D.C.

109 ANDERSEN reading aloud at Frijsenborg Manor in the summer of 1863. Odense City Museums. *Photo Royal Danish Ministry of Foreign Affairs*

110 TORCHLIGHT PROCESSION for Andersen on his appointment as honorary citizen of Odense, 6 December 1867. Fresco by Larsen Stevns. Odense City Museums. *Photo Royal Danish Ministry of Foreign Affairs*

111 THE DIPLOMA making Andersen an honorary citizen of Odense. Dated 15 November 1867. Presented to him at a banquet in Odense on 6 December 1867. Odense City Museums. *Photo Royal Danish Ministry of Foreign Affairs*

112 ANDERSEN IN OLD AGE, in his Copenhagen home. Odense City Museums. *Photo Hansen, Schou and Weller*, Copenhagen

DOROTHEA MELCHIOR. Royal Library, Copenhagen

113 ANDERSEN at Rolighed, Melchior's country house. *Photo Royal Danish Ministry of Foreign Affairs*

MORITZ MELCHIOR. Royal Library, Copenhagen

115 STATUE OF ANDERSEN in the Royal Gardens, Copenhagen. *Photo Danish Tourist Board*

INDEX

Page numbers in italics indicate illustrations

¥1000 —
4
円